the COWBOY

the COWBOY

Photography by Bank Langmore
Text by Ron Tyler

A Ridge Press Book published by
William Morrow and Company Inc., New York

TEXT CREDITS

Permission to quote material from the following sources is gratefully acknowledged:
E. C. Abbott and Helena Huntington Smith, **We Pointed Them North.**
    Norman: University of Oklahoma Press, 1954.
Will Tom Carpenter, **Lucky 7: A Cowman's Autobiography.**
    Austin: University of Texas Press, 1957.
Agnes Morley Cleaveland, **No Life for a Lady.** Boston: Houghton Mifflin Company, 1941.
Frank Collinson, Life in the Saddle, ed. and arr. by Mary Whatley Clark.
    Norman: University of Oklahoma Press, 1963.
J. Frank Dobie, **Cow People.** Boston: Little, Brown and Company, 1964.
Baylis John Fletcher, **Up the Trail in '79.** Norman: University of Oklahoma Press,
    new edition copyright, 1968.
J. Evetts Haley (ed.), "A Log of the Texas-California Cattle Trail, 1854, by James
    G. Bell," **Southwestern Historical Quarterly,** XXXV (Jan. and Apr. 1932),
    XXXVI (July, 1932), copyright by the Texas State Historical Association.
Mat Ennis Jones, **Fiddlefooted.** Denver: Sage Books, 1966.
Bob Kennon, **From the Pecos to the Powder:** A Cowboy's Autobiography.
    Norman: University of Oklahoma Press, 1965.
James Emmit McCauley, **A Stove-Up Cowboy's Story.** Dallas: Southern Methodist
    University Press, 1943. Copyright by the Texas Folklore Society.
Bart McDowell, **The American Cowboy in Life and Legend.** Washington:
    The National Geographic Society, 1972.
Walter S. Sanderlin (ed.), "A Cattle Drive from Texas to California: The Diary
    of M. H. Erskine, 1854," **Southwestern Historical Quarterly,** LXVII (Jan.
    1964). Copyright by the Texas State Historical Association.

PICTURE CREDITS

Historical photographs by Erwin E. Smith and three
    photographs by Toni Frissell on pages 132-3 reproduced by courtesy
    of the Library of Congress.
Illustrations from **Frank Leslie's Illustrated Newspaper**
    and **Harper's Weekly** are reproduced by courtesy of The Library
    Company of Philadelphia, Philadelphia, PA 19107,
    except page 46, which is courtesy
    of Sterling Memorial Library, Yale University, New Haven, CT 06520.
    Photograph page 85 (bottom) by Dorothy Langmore.

Photography on cover and title pages: ZX Ranch, Paisley, OR.

Editor-in-Chief: Jerry Mason
Editorial Director: Adolph Suehsdorf
Art Director: Albert Squillace
Managing Editor: Moira Duggan
Art Associate: David Namias
Art Production: Doris Mullane

A Ridge Press Book published by William Morrow and Company, Inc.

Library of Congress Catalog Card Number 75-10802
ISBN 0-688-02962-0

Printed and bound in Italy by Mondadori Editore, Verona.

contents

introduction

The American cowboy is a durable creature who has survived dime novels, dramatic productions, movies, television, rampant commercialization, and even scholarly investigation. He was and is a real man. He did corral long-horns and drive them up the Chisholm Trail. He did celebrate in Abilene, Dodge, or any one of a dozen other cattle towns spread from Texas to Montana. And he did become a cornerstone of America's concept of itself.

The cowboy has not died. He lives today in the West—Texas, Nevada, Montana, Wyoming, Oregon, Arizona, New Mexico, everywhere grazing land still exists. The puncher cut from the same mold as those dusty, thirsty, haggard cowboys who drove cattle up the trails to Kansas might work on a ranch in West Texas, attend the Fat Stock Show and Rodeo in Fort Worth, and herd cattle only as far as his outside fence, but his spirit remains loyal to those original cowboys who set the pattern that he admires.

To learn the story of this dwindling number of iconoclasts, I traveled to ranches and talked to contemporary cowboys. I talked with ranchers concerned about the price of beef. I talked with cowboys worried only that the open range would vanish during their lifetime. And I talked with foremen who were only too willing to confirm that genuine cowboys are increasingly hard to find. These men constitute a unique group, living with, yet minimally affected by, the twentieth-century computerization and mechanization that seems to have touched us all. They have been sympathetically, colorfully, dramatically, and truthfully filmed by Bank Langmore, himself a former cowboy who probably would spend the rest of his days in the saddle if he were permitted to use a camera instead of a rope. His pictures of the life and work of the American cowboy from 1973 to 1975 will one day constitute as useful a historic archive as those of Erwin Smith or L. A. Huffman.

In reconstructing the cowboy's story, I have relied strongly on the words and pictures of eye-witnesses: newspaper and magazine reporters who visited the first cowboys; artists attracted to the West by the dramatic nature of the frontier; photographers who thoroughly documented the cowboy's life and work. I have also used the testimony of cowboys themselves in autobiographies, diaries, journals, and correspondence. I have tried to let the cowboy speak for himself whenever possible. I have not changed the spelling or punctuation of any of the quotes (except when understanding was difficult) so as to interfere as little as possible with the directness of the cowboys' language.

I am indebted to many people for the assistance in this study, notably H. L. Kokernot, Jr., and Chris Lacy, of Alpine, Texas; Benny Binion, of Jordan, Montana, and Las Vegas, Nevada; Dr. and Mrs. Malcolm D. McLean, of Fort Worth, Texas; Mrs. Nancy Graves Wynne, Mrs. Marjorie A. Morey, and Mrs. Linda Lorenz, of the Amon Carter Museum, Fort Worth; Leonard Sanders, Jr., Fine Arts Editor of the Fort Worth **Star-Telegram;** Dr. Lawrence R. Murphy, of Western Illinois University, Macomb; and to Bank Langmore, who shared his knowledge of the range and the contemporary cowboy. My wife, Paula, gave invaluable assistance and suggestions throughout the work.

Ron Tyler

notes on the photography

With the contemporary photographs appearing in this book, I have attempted to document the American cowboy and buckaroo as he exists on large cattle ranches from Mexico to Canada in the nineteen seventies. A number of cowboy-related, ranch-hand activities have been ignored; my purpose has been to show only those unique men, descendents of the range riders of a century ago, who still make their living entirely on horseback. Photographing these men and their families, and getting to know them personally, has been the most rewarding experience of my life.

In the course of my travels, I covered about 20,000 miles of western cow country. I rode out and worked alongside cowboys during the spring and fall roundups and the times between. I had my own saddle and bedroll and everything else that makes up a cowboy's gear. After months of exposure to these men, I think I can appreciate their belief in what they do and their love for the environment in which they work. It is an inspiration in this day and age, when so many people seem unfulfilled by their jobs and lifestyles.

The physical and technical demands of the project, both on me and on my photographic equipment, were considerable. Altogether, I made some 15,000 exposures in black & white and color. There were many times, after eight to twelve hours on horseback, when I wasn't sure I could saddle up again the next morning. In fact, after several days of riding at the Four Sixes, the first outfit I visited, I was so saddle sore that I had to sleep with my hind end sticking out of my bedroll. This pleased the cowboy sense of humor, and for my part I developed a tremendous respect for the cowboy's physical endurance and capabilities.

My biggest problem was carrying all my camera gear a-horseback. I started off with two cameras swinging from each shoulder and additional film in my Levi jacket and chap pockets. I soon had bruises on my sides and back. I then had holsters made to accommodate two camera bodies, one with an 80/200mm zoom lens, the other with a 50mm. I added a couple of saddlebags, insulated against heat with foam rubber, in which I carried extra film and a 28mm lens. This was my range outfit. The camera holsters were worn like gun holsters and caused quite a bit of comment as I pulled my cameras out and started shooting.

I carried seven Minolta SRT-101 and XK camera bodies, an SRM Minolta motor drive, a Nikonos 11, a Leitz/Minolta CL, and a Zeiss Hologon camera with 15mm lens. I used a full complement of Rokkor lenses for the Minoltas, from 16 to 800mm. The lens I used most often when photographing a-horseback was the 80/200 zoom which, considering the circumstances under which some of the pictures were made—a moving horse, low light coupled with shutter speeds of 1/15 to 1/60 of a second at maximum aperture—delivered images of incredible crispness.

On the ground, the 28 F/2.5 and 100mm F/2 were most frequently used. As situations and landscape changed from ranch to ranch, I found myself using other lenses of varying focal length to capture a particular mood or perspective. The 16mm, 100mm macro, and 800mm mirror lenses proved especially worthwhile.

The justification for taking seven Minolta bodies was twofold: I had adequate backup, and the flexibility that comes with different films in different bodies. In black & white I used Kodak Panatonic X, Tri X, and 2475, as well as Ilford FP4. Color was Kodachrome 11, 25, 64, and High Speed Ektachrome. Most of the High Speed Ektachrome was push-processed to ASA 640. The black & white film was developed in Ethol TEC, Microdol X, and Acufine for the 2475.

The beating my cameras took was terrific—dust, sand, snow, rain, and a tremendous amount of vibration and jarring. During snow and extreme cold I carried the Leitz/Minolta with 40 and 90mm lenses around my neck and under a down jacket, which worked beautifully even while riding. During spring and summer heat I protected my film with insulated ice chests and bags. No film, fortunately, was ruined by heat.

I guess I can best sum up the essence of the cowboy by what Ray McLaughlin, buckaroo boss of the huge ZX Ranch, at Paisley, Oregon, said one day as his twelve buckaroos and I rode out to make the morning circle. It was dawn. The sun was still behind the mountains. We were riding at an Oregon gallop. You could hear the large-roweled buckaroo spurs jingling. I will never forget the excitement I felt. And looking at the buckaroos, I sensed the same feeling among them. At that moment Ray rode up alongside me and said, "I wonder how many people in this world would give everything they own to be riding out with us this morning?"

It is such men that this book is about. To all of them who took me in and allowed me to share their life, my deep appreciation. For one long moment I felt a very real part of it. To them and to all who share their love of the West, I dedicate the photography in this book. Long may you live, Cowboy!

—**Bank Langmore**

Warm thanks for open-handed hospitality and photographic cooperation are extended to the owners, managers, and working cowboys of the following ranches:

6666, Guthrie, TX; Quien Sabe, Channing, TX; 06, Alpine, TX; Reynolds Cattle Co., Kent, TX; Diamond A Cattle Co. (Big Bend Ranch), Presidio, TX; Bell, Bell Ranch, NM; WS, Raton, NM; Tequesquite, Albert, NM; ZX, Paisley, OR; MC, Adel, OR; Matador Cattle Co. (Quarter Circle A Ranch, Paradise Valley, NV, and Roberts Ranch, Alcova, WY); Padlock, Dayton, WY, and Crow Agency, MT; John Scott Cattle Co., Billings, MT; Horseshoe, Dayton, WY; Benny Binion, Jordan, MT; Little Horn (Antler Cattle Co.), Wyola, MT; Kramer, Cohagen, MT.

the real cowboy

Until September in 1867, the cowboy was just another over-worked ranch hand with a bad reputation. But in that month, Joseph G. McCoy opened his cattle pens in Abilene, Kansas, to Texas longhorns, and the image began to change. The cowboy who drove the steers northward to market over the Chisholm Trail rapidly attracted attention in a country recovering from a bitter civil war and looking westward for relief.

"This kind of life seems to have an inexpressible charm for the young men," exclaimed a San Antonio reporter. "It is an exciting scene to see them in full chase, with their lariats whirling over their heads, their mustangs as much excited by the race as themselves."

"Cowboys are a much misrepresented set of people," Theodore Roosevelt told a New York **Tribune** reporter in 1884. "I have taken part with them in roundups, have eaten, slept, hunted and herded cattle with them, and have never had any difficulty. If you choose to enter rum shops or go on drinking sprees with them, it is easy to get into difficulty as it would be in New York, or anywhere else . . . and there are many places in our cities where I should feel less safe than I would among the wildest cowboys in the West."

The cowboy had not always been so well thought of. The word "cowboy" had evolved from the Tory guerrillas who roamed New York State during the Revolution and cropped up again in the Texas Revolutionary Army company of 1842, but the image denoted by the word was that of "rough men with shaggy hair and wild, staring eyes." Some ranchers even refused to use the word, preferring instead the antiseptic "hands." Writers for **Harper's Weekly** and **Leslie's Illustrated,** the two most widely read weeklies of the nineteenth century, reported that the cowboy was considered "a constant source of peril to the settler and tradesman," a man with "no fear," who "respects no law." Even after the cowboy had won almost universal admiration as an American folk hero, there were outbreaks of violence that recalled their lawless days. As late as 1881, Arizona cowboys became nationally known for bandit raids, and President Chester A. Arthur denounced them as "armed desperadoes" in a message to Congress after frightened citizens of the territory telegraphed him for assistance.

But when McCoy established a market for cattle at Abilene, he gave the haphazard ranching business a large part of the stability it needed to become a viable industry, and the hard-working, hard-riding cowboy began to become respectable. By 1879, his image had picked up some of the "hero" gloss it has today. Most westerners realized that the cowboy was "just a plain, everyday bow-legged human," but his double conquest of the rangy, wild Texas longhorn and the "Great American Desert," as the Great Plains was called, imbued him with a superhuman reputation.

"There is perhaps no class of civilized beings whose characteristics are more marked than the Texas cow boy," boasted the editor of the Victoria (Texas) **Advocate.** "Accustomed to the saddle from infancy, he grows up familiar with his native prairies, and a love for them develops with his manhood, which appears to the stranger an infatuation. What the broad

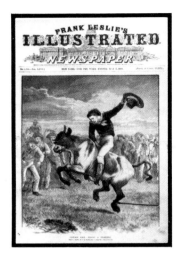

Cowboy fun—riding a yearling,
Cheyenne. WY. 1888.

ocean is to the mariner, the broad Texas prairie is to the cow boy. It is the scene of his excitements, his discoveries, and adventures. It is his couch at night, with the star-gemed vault of heaven his covering. In rain or shine, in cold or heat, he is at home among his herds, and laughs at all freaks of the elements. Brave and strong, and true, he is generous, kind and just. Quick to resent a wrong and ever ready to defend his rights, warm in his friendship, but desperate in his chastisement of an enemy."

The **Advocate** editor was probably the first to point out that "One of the most marked peculiarities in the make up of Texas cow boy's character is his incapability of surprise. You can not astonish him. Should a cow boy stake his pony and retire to rest upon his saddle blanket in the prairie, miles from any habitation, and by some means be transported in his sleep to the most active portion of Broadway, New York, he would open his eyes with perfect indifference to his magnificent surroundings, pull out his butcher knife, run his hand in his boot-leg for a shuck, begin coolly making a cigarette, and inquire for his pony." Such qualities are still respected among cowboys, who seem to feel that they lose face if they show surprise in any given situation.

Their endurance was equal to their savoir-faire. "They bivouac at night, cook their own meals, seldom enter a house, drink quantities of black coffee, generally without sugar, kill a yearling when they need meat, and are truly rough and ready riders," claimed another observer. From them "comes the noted Texas ranger, and it would be hard to find a better training for a cavalry soldier. Their splendid qualities were exhibited on many hard-fought fields during our late unpleasantness."

By 1882 the cowboy myth already had begun to get out of hand. "The cowboy of the great cattle ranges in the West and Southwest is a distinct genus," related a novice reporter for **Leslie's.** "He is unlike any other being. He enters upon his business life when he is seven years old, and in nine cases out of ten he dies a cowboy, even should he reach the age of Methuselah. His pet is his horse; his toy a revolver; a source of intense pride, his hat—a broad brimmed straw or wool affair. Leather leggins are worn over his pantaloons, and heavy top-boots, with high heels and enormous spurs,

Preceding pages: Bell cowboys tell stories and sing songs while relaxing under chuck wagon tarp before dinner. Bell is one of New Mexico's oldest and largest ranches, originally was a Spanish land grant.

Skinning a beef on the range.

protect his feet." In town the cowboys reportedly behaved like the ruffians of earlier fame. "Two or three will dash through a town, and, before the people know what is going on will have robbed every store of importance and made their escape. Two have defied successfully a dozen constables, and a score could circumvent an entire company of militia."

Visitors to the West emphasized the yarns, but also noted a few touches of reality. E. C. ("Teddy Blue") Abbott, an Englishman turned cowboy, remembered the loneliness of the trail when men "told each other everything we knew in a week." Soon even the songs grew tiresome and good humor vanished. "After that it was nothing but sowbelly and beans, three times a day." Another observer of hundreds of ranches recalled that the men were so bored that they often memorized the labels on canned goods, then recited them to their surprised visitors without warning or request. "Condensed milk is prepared from . . .," went one ditty, while "Of Peaches" was the favorite on another ranch.

The most evident quality of cowboying—hard work—should have surfaced more quickly. Some authors did consider the chores difficult and numerous, but quickly moved on to the assertion that the freedom, fun, and swashbuckling more than made up for the hardness of life. Charles A. Siringo romanticized his **Fifteen Years on the Hurricane Deck of a Spanish Pony** for hundreds of thousands of readers beginning in 1885 and continuing through numerous editions, but he always said his excuse for writing the book was "money—and lots of it." So he wrote what he thought would sell, and he got his ideas of salability from the **Police Gazette.**

The cowboy's public image rapidly attracted other propagandists. Owen Wister, who at one point doubted the cowboy's morality, recanted to the extent of creating the stereotypical cowboy hero in his novel, **The Virginian.** Published in 1902, this was the first cowboy novel and one of the best-selling western books of all time—more than 1,600,000 copies sold in the United States alone. By 1885, he wrote, the "eastern notion of the West was 'Alkali Ike' and smoking pistols." Untried youngsters departed the farms and signed their names on the roll books of such famous ranches as the XIT, the Spur, and the Matador. Naive Englishmen left stodgy offices on Bond Street to take up the lariat, and easterners like Roosevelt revived their health on western ranches. The word "cowboy" had added another meaning: virtually anyone who rode a western pony or owned part of a ranch.

Soon the cowboy's defenders took up the fight. This word cowboy "is not intended to apply to all men who have taken an active part in handling cattle, but to those only who have proven themselves worthy the name of genuine," declared Will S. James, the cowboy preacher from Texas who set down his hard-earned opinions on the subject in 1893. He further divided cowboys into three classes. Number one, the genuine cowboy "because of his true manhood." Number two is "worth consideration," says James, because he is the "true type of western hospitality" and is "liberal to a fault." Number three is, perhaps, the most popular description of a cowboy: the "roaming, 'come day, go day, God send Sunday, good-natured easy-going cow-boy,' who is just as happy where he is as where he is not; who cares for nothing but a good saddle, spurs and quirt and a forty dollar job." In conclusion, wrote James, "my definition of the cow-boy is a big-hearted, whole-souled bundle of humanity, kind-hearted, generous to a fault, possessed of all the frailties common to mankind, and not the biggest rascal on the earth by a jug full."

All other pretenders James ruled out, saying that they were fakes and frauds, pretending to the honorable name of cowboy, a name which had become honorable only within two decades of James' writing. James began the discussion of what or who is the real cowboy, a topic that has endured until today and probably will persist as long as "Americans" are considered.

Two Ivy League-educated easterners tossed their contributions into the corporate image of the real cowboy late in the last century. According to Teddy Roosevelt and Frederic Remington, both of whom owned western ranches at one time and spent a considerable amount of their time with cowboys, the cowboy was a man. Others could be men, of course, but the cowboy was the perfect specimen, the combination of the best ingredients that made the western man. Some think Roosevelt glorified the cowboy when he spoke of the Dakota Bad Lands as being "overwhelmingly masculine . . . a product of their environment and a prerequisite for success in coping with it." "With me," wrote Remington after decades of interpreting the puncher in paint, "cowboys are what gems and porcelains are to others."

While many amateur pundits have claimed that the cowboy had to have "horse sense," or logic, Wister imbued his hero with raw intelligence. Wister's cowboy reeked of roughness to the eastern maiden he respected, but possessed immense amounts of native ability, quickly absorbed the books she loaned him, and eventually proved her equal in literary discussions.

It was rather natural that a man possessing courage, manliness, horsemanship, liberality, and intelligence should become a folk hero. The cowboy's chief publicist was Ned Buntline (nee Edward Zane Carroll Judson), who wrote dozens of dime novels. Buntline published a sensational story about William F. ("Buffalo Bill") Cody in 1869 which was so successful that he soon had Cody, an authentic frontiersman, on the melodrama stage acting out his novels. Buffalo Bill quickly developed a feel for showmanship that enabled him to continue to publicize the West on his own. Organizing his

19

Holding an early morning
herd prior to branding
on land leased from Crow Indian
Reservation by Little
Horn Ranch (Antler Cattle Co.), MT.
This is some of best pasture
in West. Opposite: Neighboring
ranch owner shows
up to help spring roundup
at Four Sixes, Guthrie, TX.

Wild West Show in 1883, Cody took good horsemen across America and Europe, spreading the growing legends of the American West. Cody's cowboys were excellent riders, but they were more: they were good shots, good showmen.

But even Cody, who had set out with the noble goal of showing the world how it was in the real West, soon fell to publicity gimmicks and stunts designed to draw a crowd rather than depict the authentic West. From good intentions, accurate knowledge, and famous incidents in Western history, Cody went to myth with stars like Annie "Little Sure Shot" Oakley, Chief Iron Tail of "Buffalo" nickle fame, and Johnny Baker, the "Cowboy Kid." Bill's troupe "reenacted" the ride of the Deadwood stagecoach, complete with a savage Indian attack and the last minute rescue by the cavalry. They defended hearth and home as the Indians attacked the settler's cabin, driving the innocent family from its homestead, only to be saved again in the last instant by the "bluecoats." Bill even admitted that one of the most famous of the melodrama plays written for him—a story honoring his real-life taking of the first scalp in revenge for Colonel George A. Custer's massacre—was not historically accurate. "It was a five-act play without head or tail," he said, "and it made no difference at which act we commenced the performance."

The cowboy's manly image has been solidified and enhanced in the twentieth century by motion pictures. From **The Great Train Robbery** of 1903 onward, there have been movies about virtually every aspect of the cowboy's story.

Much of the publicity, however, distorts the historical accuracy of the cowboy's image. The cowboy seems to be the fundamental character around which many American values are constructed—the strong man at the bottom of the pyramid of other less-popular western types, like the cavalryman, the teamster, the badman. In the process he has absorbed elements of all their characters until little remains intact but his machismo. Today the cowboy's image is mingled with—and partakes of—those of rancher, badman, gambler, Indian fighter, stage driver, marshal, and hired gunslinger. This clearly is not the authentic cowboy that Joseph McCoy introduced to the world in 1867.

After such expert tampering, even the real punchers of today convey a diffused image. Some dress in the manner of the dude of several generations ago. Others slouch about, feeling that their authenticity is certified by their rough-out boots, crumpled hat, or red bandana. The western image has attracted imposters, and even those who should know stammer while attempting to describe the real cowboy. Today's cowmen are proud creatures, knowledgeable of their heritage and aspiring to continue it. They have read the dozens of recent books about their kind and seen all the movies. They have absorbed the romantic television dramas and laughed at the ignorant mistakes, such as "cowboys" in bib overalls driving fence posts into the ground with a sledge hammer. The cowboys generally want the image honed to its realities, whatever they be, because they love the life they lead and relish its accurate depiction.

One strong, tall Montana cowboy of today has definite

Left to right, top to bottom: Rough-string rider (horse breaker) for ZX, Paisley, OR; ranch manager, 06's, Alpine, TX; buckaroo, MC Ranch, Adel, OR; manager and hand, Horseshoe Ranch, Dayton, WY; 6666's cowboy; Padlock (WY) cowboy; ZX buckaroo.

23

"Capture of a Texas town by cowboys." 1882 **Leslie's** shows cowboys on the kinds of tear that made them feared by residents of small western towns.

opinions about the real cowboy. The modern-day puncher is different from his historic cousin in many ways, but essentially they are the same according to Bud, who has spent most of his fifty-three years in the saddle. A soft-spoken man whose words carry the conviction of years of experience and the authority that glistens from his squinty eyes, Bud contends that a cowboy has "to be able to ride and rope, and to know horses and cows. You have to know how to pick out a good horse and learn his habits. A good cowboy can look just awful if he don't know his horse, or if he is on a nag." Bud's conditions for admission as a genuine puncher are simple. A cowboy must have split-second reaction, strength, and ability that comes only with the same constant practice that Bud has invested during his years of quiet intensity.

Knowledge of horses is one of the characteristics necessary in any outstanding cowboy. Teddy Blue Abbott, who rode the same Montana range a century ago, would have agreed with Bud, but he would have added independence, not to say stubbornness, to the list. A real cowboy took care of his string of horses and was proud of them. The foreman assigned each rider a string of six to eight ranch horses for the roundup and trail that were his to ride and look after for the season. Horses and men got to know each other, and the cowboys made certain that each horse was worked equally. The relationship developed to the point that when Conrad Kohrs, the president of the HDS Cattle Company, asked his foreman to get him a horse to ride for the day, and the foreman went to one of the cowboys and asked for a horse, the man replied, "Hell, no! He can't ride none of my horses." The cowboy was standing up for his rights, according to the code of the range, even though the horses belonged to the ranch.

Perhaps the most important attribute of a real cowboy remains unsaid by the generations of historians, novelists, and screen writers. To many the cowboy not only must be western, but he must be the epitome of American. The Idea of Progress, which holds that man improves simply by existing through time, and Frederick Jackson Turner's Frontier Thesis, which attempts to explain the development of American democracy in terms of the western advance, are wedded in the manufacture of the cowboy, creating a new society and, in St. John Crèvecoeur's phrase, a "new man." The cowboy, riding one of nature's noblest creatures, the wild mustang, across the arid Plains with hundreds of the surliest animals, the Texas longhorns, in front of him, emerged as the best known synthesis of values described by Turner and Crèvecoeur as American.

There is another element the real cowboy must have

today that did not affect the cowboy of yesterday. "It is in your mind," said Bud emphatically. "You have to think like a cowboy to be a cowboy. Today a man might do the work of a cowboy, but if he don't think like a cowboy, he's not a cowboy. You have to hold to the old ways." In a world burgeoning with pickup trucks, scientific feeding, and the pressures of a modern market, this is a difficult and iconoclastic pursuit, but there is still a place for the authentic cowboy. Not all have to change to fit a "modern" rancher's concept of today's cowboy.

Of course, the original cowboys did not have to "hold to the old ways," because they created them. Nor was there any set pattern. The characteristics of the cowboy and the job developed through twenty years of trail driving from 1867 until 1887 or 1890. The final evolutionary product of both cowboy and job are today understood to be the way it was throughout the twenty years or so of development, but the patterns and characteristics are much more fluid than some histories would have you believe.

Handling horses and cattle was the absolute essential requirement for a cowboy. Then, he had to accompany the animals on a long trail drive to market, or, later, he had to ride a train on which the cattle were shipped. After the blizzard of 1886-87 in Montana, ranchers turned to storing hay so they would have adequate forage for the winter, and the cowboy was forced into yet another undreamed-of job. Instead of sitting around a warm fireplace during the winter months, he had to pitch hay to the hungry cattle so they could survive until spring. After termination of the trail drives, cowboys spent the entire year on the ranch if they were full-time hands, or if they were seasonal employees they worked at some related task. Thus it became increasingly difficult even for real cowboys to "hold to the old ways."

In truth, there is little excuse for an unauthentic portrait of the genuine western American cowboy, because his history is so thoroughly documented that a quick trip to almost any library will produce more material than the average reader can consume in weeks. Newspaper reporters traversed the West, pencil ready, imagination fervid, and sketch pad in hand. Intelligent, articulate ranchers like Charles Goodnight talked to historians who had the rare ability to capture their essence in a book, and rancher-businessmen like John Clay penned their own memoirs. Artists Frederic Remington and Charles M. Russell saw the real West before it fled before civilization, and Frank Tenny Johnson, W. H. D. Koener, and Olaf Selzer followed in their wake, painting virtually every facet of the cattlemen/punchers. Photographers packed their heavy cameras and fragile glass-plate negatives into the outback, followed crews on roundups, and rushed through rivers and over hills to get to the other side in time to catch the cattle coming through. Novelists like Andy Adams and Owen Wister left accurate records and thoughtful interpretations of the cowboy and his friends, and historians seem to have almost exhausted the relevant materials in writing biographies, histories of ranches, and memoirs of the old timers. Perhaps the difficulty in determining the real from the imagined is the superfluity rather than deficiency of information. The cowboy is best presented when allowed to speak for himself, in words or pictures. This is a real portrait.

the development of ranching

Ranching is a world-wide industry; the American West has no monopoly. Although laced with different customs and folklore, ranching in its basic form evolved wherever men worked cattle from horseback: the western United States, Brazil and Argentina, Australia, and Saudi Arabia, for example. The four basic elements that combined to produce the ranches of the American West are common to all ranching situations: cattle, horses, land, and men. The man on horseback is the most constant element wherever ranching sprang up, but the American cowboy is the best known and most popular of them all.

The well-known story of how cattle and horses got to America is that Columbus brought them to his island paradise in Santo Domingo on his second voyage in 1493. Gregorio de Villalobos transferred them to Mexico just a year after Hernando de Cortez conquered the Aztecs in 1520, and within a few months Cortez had begun raising cattle on his estate at Cuernavaca, symbolically translated from the Spanish as "cow horn."

The Spanish cattle adapted to their new environment with an ease that Columbus, Cortez, and Villalobos could neither have hoped for nor predicted. When Francisco Vázquez de Coronado gathered supplies for his 1540 exploration into the American Southwest, which was only nineteen years after cattle had been introduced to the mainland, he had no difficulty rounding up 500 cattle in Mexico.

Sixty years later he could have rounded up his cattle en route. Lower Sonora teemed with cattle by 1560. The neighboring states of Durango and Chihuahua counted herds as large as 10,000, while one rancher in the state of Jalisco branded 30,000 calves a year—a large number even in the heyday of ranching, let alone the seventeenth century. Even the unsettled portions of the country became populated with wild cattle because numbers of domesticated cattle escaped from the Spanish ranches and fled into the unexplored Southwest, where they grew wilder with each succeeding generation. So many wild cattle roamed the countryside by 1555 that ranchers were able to round up for a bullfight in honor of the new viceroy many twenty-year-old bulls that had never seen a man.

We have the Spaniards to thank for the hordes of wild livestock roaming the West in the eighteenth century. As they ventured northward from the Mexican border states of Sonora, Chihuahua, and Nuevo León, they brought their herds in increasing numbers. They took cattle into the Santa Cruz, San Pedro, and Sonoita river valleys of southern Arizona. They landed cattle on the coast of California in 1769, when the **San Carlos** docked with its settlers and supplies. The first herds probably belonged to the mission fathers, but by 1800 there were over a million head of cattle in southern California.

Because ranching was the most prosperous occupation in California, the colonial government encouraged it, granting newcomers a league of land, approximately 4,438 acres, if they provided a house and a herd of about 100 cattle. By the time of Mexican independence from Spain in 1821, California probably was the largest nonnomadic pastoral society to exist, de-

Opening pages: Holding herd in dust storm at 6666's. Opposite: Hell's Half Acre, ranch house west of Pecos, near Big Bend, one of last big range areas in Texas.

pending upon the sale of hides and tallow for its economic underpinning. During the peak year of 1838, energetic merchants in Los Angeles, San Diego, and Monterey shipped more than 200,000 hides to Boston alone. The basic social unit of the **rancho** society was the family, presided over by a patriarch who often fathered twenty or more children. By the time of the Mexican-United States war in 1846, the population of California had increased from some 3,700 to almost 8,000. Ranching had permeated the province's culture, dominating it economically and socially, until annexation by the United States in 1850. Even then, the discovery of gold in 1848 had only slightly altered the structure.

The great demand for beef for the gold miners coincided with a period of abundant rainfall and beautiful weather to usher in a prosperous era for livestock producers. Within a few years Californians had glutted the market with fat, healthy cattle that could not be sold. The decline of the cattle market and the increase in gold output radically changed the face of the state in the ensuing decades.

Cattle were also the mainstay of the Texas missions. Captain Alonso de León brought the first cattle, horses, and oxen with him in 1690 to establish Mission San Francisco de los Tejas in East Texas. Hoping to keep the basic herd intact and use only the "increase" for sustenance for the natives, Domingo Terán brought other livestock to the mission the following year. The Indians stole many animals from the original seed herd of 200, but within twenty years the Spaniards had herds grazing the rich Texas grass from the Neches to the Trinity rivers.

The friars and mission Indians apparently were good cowboys, for the herds increased. From 3,000 in 1758 the herd at Mission Espíritu Santo, near Goliad, grew to more than 16,000 by 1768. In 1779 Athanase de Mézières, a Frenchman in the service of Spain, observed that, "the increase of our stock has been so great that though there has been difficulty in selling and negligence in caring for them, we can secure those which we would devote to breeding and use from the Guadalupe, San Marcos, Las Animas, Colorado, San Xavier, San Andrés, and the Brazos" rivers.

As the province was stocked, three major ranching areas developed: San Antonio, Nacogdoches, and the region between the Rio Grande and the Nueces River. The migration northward began when forty-six-year-old Tomás Sánchez settled Laredo in 1755. Similar land grants were given to other Mexican **empresarios** in the ensuing years, and when Fray Juan Agustín Morfi was in Texas in 1777 and 1778 he counted seventeen **ranchos** along the San Antonio River alone. By 1800 there were forty-five in the state.

Although not as luxurious as life on the Mexican **hacienda,** life on a Texas **rancho** was good for the seventeenth- and eighteenth-century frontier. Since **peons** or Indian slaves were not available in Texas, the **rancho** depended upon a self-sufficient family unit. Whereas the **hacienda** contained a church, a chaplain, a peasant village, and often thousands of people, the **rancho** was much smaller and was worked by the family. The life of Don Luciano García, a former Texas governor, seemed idyllic to James Austin, brother of Stephen F., one of the first Texas **empresarios,** when he visited the San Carlos, Tamaulipas, **rancho** in 1826. He "is a perfect hermit," wrote Austin. "Since his return from Bexar he has resided at his **Rancho de la Luz:** rarely has communication with any one, except his Vaceros . . . Spends good part of his time Sleeping and eating."

The Anglo-Americans had known about the cattle and horse herds in Texas long before the Austins brought the original 300 families to settle. Philip Nolan, prototype for "the man without a country," had been killed near present-day Waco in 1801, while on his third horse-hunting expedition from nearby Louisiana. Stephen F. Austin began bringing his colonists into the state in the early 1820s, each settler bringing five or ten milch cows with him.

Austin, in fact, considered taking up ranching in 1826 had he been unable to bring any more families into the province. Writing to Juan Antonio Padilla, Texas Secretary of State, he mentioned that he sent his brother James to Tamaulipas to search for cattle and horses to buy, and that he was considering starting a **"ranchito,"** even though "by necessity I will have to learn how to operate a ranch and care for cattle." Austin's brother shared the same dream. Reporting on his trip to Tamaulipas, he wrote: "I flatter myself that in a short time we shall have a smug little **Rancho**—then you or myself (or both of us) must get a **wife** and forget the cares and perplexities of the world, in the pleasures to be found in a **Pastoral life."**

The Americans in Austin's colony enjoyed the same success with cattle raising that the Spaniards did. The Kuykendall family, which started in 1822 with a herd of seventy, had increased it to more than 2,000 by 1837. Herds in Austin's colony had increased from an estimated 3,500 in 1826 to more than 26,000 in 1831. An 1837 traveler reported that several colonists near Houston owned herds of 500 to 4,000, and that "immense herds" roamed the bottom land near the Brazos River.

Cowpunchers "hightailing it in to chuck" on OR range, Arizona, 1909.

Across the Rio Grande:
Cantina at Boquillas and
vaquero by simple hitching
post at San Vicente
look like predecessors
of a century ago.
South of these border
towns are some of
Mexico's largest haciendas.

33

Austin's colonists were not the only cattle raisers in Anglo-American Texas. The Atascosita District, between the Austin Colony and the Louisiana border, was the home of squatters who had no legal right to the land, but who had simply drifted across the Sabine River and settled in the less inhabited areas. By 1850 more than 4,000 persons lived there, many of whom were cattle raisers. They might have owned more cattle than the members of Austin's colony, in fact, for the 1834 census showed more than 50,000 cattle in the Department of Nacogdoches, which included Atascosita. An 1850 traveler in the region noted "cattle of the finest kind, several hundreds together and thousands in some places."

Although there were several ranching centers in the state, cattle raising soon concentrated in a diamond-shaped area of South Texas running from San Antonio to Laredo to Brownsville to Indianola and back to San Antone. One historian has called it "the primary nursery and stronghold of the longhorn." After the Texas fight for independence in 1836, the region became a no-man's land claimed by both Texas and Mexico but possessed by neither. After passing through it, James Austin wrote his brother that, "I shall know how to justly appreciate the fertility of our . . . soil." But the cattle prospered on the grass that stayed green all year long, and a slow westward migration began. The 1840 tax list of Texas shows that fifty percent of the 125,000 cattle in the state were located in the coastal prairie. By 1845 that percentage had declined to forty percent of some 336,000 cattle, and to only thirty percent of the total in 1850.

Because of the character of the land, the cattle bred without interference. The fact that the Spaniards did not castrate their bulls meant that wild herds bred from escaped bulls throughout the state. The "no-man's" character of the land kept settlers from it for a few years, and because it was located east of San Antonio, on the edge of the frontier, Indians to the west did not molest the cattle. The herds grew in numbers and in fierceness. Colonel Richard Irving Dodge related an incident that occurred when General Zachary Taylor was marching his army from Corpus Christi through the heart of the diamond region to Matamoros in 1846. "A soldier on the flank of the column . . . fired at a bull," wrote Dodge. "The bull immediately charged, and the soldier . . . ran into the column. The bull . . . charged headlong, scattering several regiments like chaff, and finally escaped unhurt, having demoralised and put to flight an army which a few days after covered itself with glory by victoriously encountering five times its numbers of human enemies [at Palo Alto, near Brownsville, in the first battle of the war with Mexico]."

Only the most adventurous immigrants, such as Thomas O'Connor from Ireland, got grants west of Austin's colony. O'Connor was given more than 4,000 acres in what is today Refugio County, near Victoria, Texas. He gradually increased the size of his ranch, recording his THC brand in 1848, and accumulating more than 40,000 cattle by 1862. Soon the leading newspaper of the state had written about his "princely estate" on the San Antonio River. Shipping cattle from the port of Indianola to market in New Orleans, O'Connor ultimately built a ranch of more than half a million acres.

Coming from the urban center of New York City was

Preceding pages: Moving cattle
into pens for branding, Quien Sabe
Ranch, Channing, TX. Top:
Roping strayed calf. Opposite: Muley
(dehorned) cow, 6666's. Above:
Horned Herefords, Quien Sabe.
Ranches differ on horns.
Dehorned cattle transport better,
fit in feedlots better, are less
prone to injury. But horned
animals don't bunch, are easier to rope.
Cowboys say dehorned cow
is a poor mother. Cutting horns
''cuts her brains out.''

Manuel Carillo,
Mexican vaquero,
waters his horses
in Rio Grande. Mexico
is at right,
Texas at left.

Richard King, another who adopted Texas as his residence and moved into the diamond-shaped area of cattle raising after the Mexican War ended in 1848. In 1853 he purchased Santa Gertruda, a 75,000-acre Spanish land grant. With his partner, Mifflin Kenedy, King prospered by trading cotton to Mexico during the Civil War, then used that profit to buy more South Texas ranch land. The giant King Ranch is the result of his shrewd management.

Certain characteristics of the longhorn breed were becoming evident in 1845, when a Houston newspaper editor described the cattle running near the sources of the San Gabriel and Brushy creeks. "They differ in form, color and habits from all the varieties of domestic cattle in Texas," he noted. "They are invariably of a dark brown color, with a slight tinge of dusky yellow on the tip of the nose and on the belly. Their horns are remarkably large, and stand out straight from the head. Although these cattle are generally much larger than the domestic cattle, they are more fleet and nimble, and when pursued, often outstrip horses that easily outrun the buffalo. . . . It is said that their fat is so hard and compact that it will not melt in the hottest days of summer; and the candles formed with it are far superior to those that are formed with the tallow of other cattle." By 1866 there were an estimated 3,500,000 to 4,500,000 such cattle in Texas.

Horses were brought to the New World from England, France, and Holland, as well as Spain, but northern European steeds did not get into the early West. The wild mustang of the prairie that became the constant companion of the cowboy and inspired countless artists in their attempt to depict his spirit and freedom had a similar origin to the longhorn, though his character seemed to be one part nobility and another part energy, while the longhorn was seldom thought of in terms other than wild and durable. The western horse's forebears accompanied the cattle across the Atlantic on Columbus' second voyage. They spread to the mainland more rapidly than the cattle, because of their importance in the conquest. Following the Spanish occupation of Mexico, the Council of the Indies—the governing body for Spain's American possessions—selected livestock to be taken to Mexico and bred. Some wealthy ranchers even imported Arabian horses in later years to improve their stock.

The product of natural selection and purposeful breeding, the Spanish horse, such as the Andalusian, soon developed an outstanding reputation. Although the twenty lancers with Columbus had traded their purebred horses for "plugs" before they left for Spain, they had secured horses which they correctly believed would make the voyage better than the high-strung steeds. Only the fittest survived the trip, meaning that the stronger horses were left to breed in the New World. Even the founding fathers of the United States were aware of the superior breed being produced in New Spain. Patrick Henry instructed Colonel George Rogers Clark to bring him back several Spanish horses while Clark was on a mission in the Old Northwest Territory, and Thomas Jefferson asked Philip Nolan to secure horses for him in Texas.

The Spanish horse found the terrain and climate in the Southwest similar to the arid lands and weather of Andalusia, in southern

Spain. Coronado was able to gather 1,500 horses for his expedition into the Southwest after only twenty years of breeding and importation into New Spain. One of the first actions of any Spanish general was to establish a **hacienda** for his livestock. So rapid was the spread of horses throughout America that they had reached Canada by the mid-eighteenth century. The Spaniards called the horses **mesteños,** which the Americans soon corrupted to "mustang."

The wild mustangs were notoriously difficult to capture, and the mustangers, or horse hunters, delighted in coming up with unique methods. The commonest ploy was inherited from the **vaqueros,** who divided into groups and drove the horses into a carefully concealed pen. Zebulon M. Pike, who witnessed a roundup when he was in Texas in 1806, said that the Spaniards took their fastest horses into "wild horse country," where they built the corral in a spot hidden by brush and trees. After they had driven the mustangs into the pen they selected the "handsomest and youngest" to keep and let the others go. "For this business," Pike concluded, "I presume there is no nation in the world superior to the Spaniards of Texas."

The Anglo-Americans contributed "walking down" to the repertory of mustangers' tricks. Hearing of a mustang the Mexicans called "the Ghost," Frank Collinson, a West Texas rancher, decided to have the horse for himself. Gathering several friends for the hunt, Collinson set out in pursuit of the Ghost and his **manada,** or herd. The riders took turns chasing the horses, neither allowing them to eat, water, or sleep. After four days of constant pursuit, the Ghost was isolated on a twenty-foot bluff overlooking Yellow House Lake, an alkali bog similar to quicksand in consistency. At first Collinson thought the horse was confused. But "I suddenly understood the animal's free, intelligent spirit," he later wrote. "I knew that the noble horse would prefer death to capture." The Ghost jumped off the bluff into the bog and slowly sank to his death.

Some hunters believed the best way to capture a mustang was to crease him with rifle fire. If the marksman could graze the spinal nerve at the top of the neck, the horse would be stunned and could be tied up before he regained his senses. Most often, however, the horse was killed by a poor shot rather than stunned by a good one. Only the most expert sharpshooter could graze the nerve cord with any consistency.

Blindfolded horses being ridden full tilt at wall to teach obedience to rider's signals. Lower (Baja) California, 1874.

Other mustangers had more unique methods of capture. Jack Thorp, a New Mexico cattleman, told of meeting a Mexican family in South Texas that chased mustangs each year. The family sometimes drove the horses into corrals, but more spectacularly, they also rode them down. Thorp watched a fourteen-year-old girl urge her horse up beside a racing mustang, then slide onto the mustang's back, slip a horsehair rope over his nose, and ride him until he was exhausted.

The most unusual mustanger of them all might have been Bob Lemmons, an ex-slave from Texas. "I acted like a mustang," he told J. Frank Dobie, who interviewed him in 1931. "I made the mustangs think I was one of them." Lemmons began by following a **manada** for several days. When the horses allowed him to approach, he made no effort to run or capture any of them. He slept and traveled with them. After about a week, Lemmons insisted, the mustangs would follow him, and he could simply lead them into a corral. "Show them you're the boss. That's the secret," he advised.

The most famous—and most difficult to capture—of the wild mustangs was the Pacing White Steed of the Prairies, a mustang that existed apparently in every region of wild horses. Since white mustangs were not terribly rare, the legends relating to the Pacing White Steed almost certainly are associated with dozens of different horses, although many old-timers chose to believe in one superhorse. The Pacing White Steed was first mentioned in literature in 1832, when Washington Irving wrote of seeing him near the Red River. He was again reported in 1844 by George Wilkins Kendall and Josiah Gregg, who published classic memoirs of their experiences in the Southwest. Numerous stories of his origin exist, as do declarations of his capture.

One of the most famous to be called the Pacing Steed ranged the San Antonio area. A team of mustangers chased him for 200 miles hoping to claim a $500 reward placed on the horse's head by a local connoisseur of horseflesh. A **vaquero** who saw the horse, jaded and exhausted, taking a drink of water, finally captured him. Rather than eat or drink in captivity, however, the horse died. Legends of the Pacing White Steed continued, symbolizing the nobility and love of freedom that the wild mustang represents today.

The Texas mustang was a noble animal, but looked more

43

like a stocky pony and made a poor work horse. Averaging from fourteen to fifteen hands in height (fifty-six to sixty inches), the mustang, however, made a superior saddle horse with good endurance. A historian who observed Sonorian mustangs for eleven years during the eighteenth century classified them as traveling horses and field horses, or cow horses, as they became known. The mustangs multiplied so rapidly that in 1829 Stephen Austin penned across the western portion of his map of Texas, "Immense Herds of Wild Horses."

If anything, the Californians were more accustomed to good horses than the Texans. Californians developed their own breed of mustang, similar to but still different from the one in Texas. Fitting the leisurely life style that distinguished the Californians from all other Spanish groups in North America, the California mustang was an important part of the culture. The men worked in the saddle, played in the saddle—even ate in the saddle. They "appeared to be always on horseback," wrote Charles Dana in **Two Years Before the Mast.**

Perhaps the most famous California horses were the two **canelos,** cinnamons or red roans, that John C. Frémont rode in 1847. In the midst of an almost miraculous nine-day trip that covered 840 miles from Los Angeles to Monterey and back, Frémont rode one **canelo** forty miles one day and ninety the next. Although the horse showed no fatigue, Frémont changed to the other one for the ride into San Luis Obispo. Reportedly the horse was still pulling at the bit when they entered the city thirty miles later, and the other one led the remuda.

The area around Los Angeles that now has more cars than probably any other spot on earth at one time led in the number of horses. They were a superior breed adapted to the luxurious grasslands of the West Coast, but had no influence in the development of the mustang of the Plains, because the mountains and desert prevented them from migrating.

The cowboy came to share the mustang's love of freedom and open spaces, and probably would have agreed with the Houston editor who commented in 1840: "When mounted on a noble animal, our concepts are bold, and we feel nerved for feats of high daring; but astride of a scrub, our

mental operations are spiritless, and creep as sluggishly as the dull animal we are riding."

Most people think of the West in terms of its spectacular landscape, such as the Grand Canyon of the Snake River or the canyon lands of Utah and Arizona, but in reality the ranching industry developed amid more mundane circumstances. The heart of cow country is the Great Plains, which encompasses all or part of all the present-day western states. An area of 900,000 square miles, the Plains is a rolling country that is comparatively flat and has few trees and insufficient rainfall for intensive agriculture. It begins approximately at the ninety-eighth meridian, which cuts through the southern portion of Texas, where many historians contend that the modern-day ranch was born. It extends through the central parts of Oklahoma, Kansas, and Nebraska, and the eastern portions of North and South Dakota. The Plains lacks minerals; the rivers are unsuited for navigation, in many instances contain quicksand, and are unfit for drinking because of the many chemicals in them.

The great natural resource of the Plains is grass, the ingredient that sustained the large midwestern cattle, horse, and buffalo herds. From the moment that Coronado described the Plains of Kansas, men knew that grass grew there in abundant quantities, but were not certain that it could be put to any good use. "It would not be possible to establish a settlement here," Coronado wrote the king, "for besides being 400 leagues from the North [Atlantic] sea and more than 200 from the South [Pacific] sea, with which it is impossible to have any sort of communication, the country is so cold . . . that apparently the winter could not possibly be spent here, because there is no wood, nor cloth with which to protect the men, except the skins which the natives wear and some small amount of cotton cloaks." Coronado was totally wrong on his estimates of distance, but his report had the effect of discouraging Spanish settlement of the area.

Nor did men readily change their minds about the Plains. Major Stephen H. Long, the first American to explore and report on the Great Plains, earned his niche in history when he coined the phrase that continued to damn it for decades: "The Great American Desert." But he found others

Horse wrangler (l) returns Bell Ranch remuda from early morning watering. Cowboys have already picked first mounts of the day and are working cattle.

45

San Antonio "herdsmen" of 1859. A
very early look at Texas vaqueros.
Note woolly chaps and decorated
stirrups. Traditional cowboy
hat has not yet evolved.

willing to support his contention. Debating whether the postal service should
be expanded to the Pacific Ocean, Daniel Webster asked his fellow congress-
men, "What do we want with this vast worthless area? This region of savages
and wild beasts, of deserts, shifting sands and whirlwinds of dust, of cactus
and prairie dogs?" Horace Greeley condemned the Plains in the New York
Tribune when he wrote that it was the "acme of barrenness and desolation,"
but perhaps the most widely read verdict was historian Francis Parkman's:
"No living thing was moving throughout that vast landscape, except the
lizards that darted over the sand and through the rank grass and prickly pears
at our feet. Before and behind us, the level monotony of the plain was un-
broken as far as the eye could reach. Sometimes it glared in the sun, an
expanse of hot, bare sand; sometimes it was veiled by coarse grass. Skulls and
whitening bones of buffalo were scattered everywhere."

Still the grass was there, a vast national treasure waiting
to be used by the gimlet-eyed cattlemen who harnessed the wild mustang and
longhorn, and penetrated the American Desert. Grass covered the Texas
prairies, along the Gulf Coast, in South Texas, and on the High Plains of West
Texas. It was good grass that stretched through the coastal prairie from the
Sabine to the Guadalupe River in southeast Texas. Early travelers referred to a
"dense mat of grass" and noted that the vegetation was so salty that the
cattle's diet did not have to be supplemented. So fertile was the ground and
hearty the grass that settlers found as early as 1824 that they could burn it in
the winter to get rid of the weeds and yet be assured of grass six inches high by
March and nearly as high as the horses' knees by the summer. The grass of
the coastal prairie provided fodder for the cattle ten months out of the year.
For the other two months the cattle foraged among the canebreaks that lined
the southeasterly coursing streams of the coastline.

Grass was also the dominant resource of the South Texas
"diamond" and remained green there all year long. The ground was comparatively level and fertile, with few trees. Rivers cut diagonally across it en route
to the Gulf and provided adequate water. Although Mark Twain was writing of
Nevada, he might have been referring to South Texas when he wrote that,
"Sometimes we have the seasons in their regular order, and then again we
have winter all summer and summer all winter." Stiff northers—winds bear-

46

ing freezing rain and sleet—are a common occurrence throughout Texas, although temperatures are generally mild. "It is mighty regular about not raining," Twain continued, "though . . . the climate is good, what there is of it."

The fact that the industries of the East were unsuited for the Great Plains led to development of the fourth element in ranching—the cowboy. "The physical conditions which exist in that land, and which inexorably control the operations of men, are such that the industries of the West are necessarily unlike those of the East, and their institutions must be adapted to their industrial wants," wrote John Wesley Powell, a great American explorer who had spent much of his time in the West. "It is thus that a new phase of Aryan civilization is being developed in the western half of America." The new industry suited to the Plains was ranching, and the new man was the cowboy. Ranching took advantage of the vast, natural grasslands, did not demand too much water, and prospered in the subhumid climate.

The cowboy was a unique institution combining the characteristics of the Mexican vaquero and the American "cow boy." Both cultures had developed sophisticated methods of handling cattle from horseback by 1836. The Spanish names and methods are perhaps better known, but the Americans applied a different vocabulary to essentially similar jobs. Whereas the Spaniards had their roundups, the Americans had their "cow hunts." Both raised cattle on the open range, causing an early traveler to lament that the cattle around Galveston were "nearly as wild as the . . . buffaloes," and another to complain that the colonists were "suffering [their cattle] to roam at large in the wilderness," like the Spanish cattle.

The similarities between the two ranching methods went deeper than working cattle from horseback, running them on the open range, and rounding them up. An 1835 observer made one of the earliest reports on branding, noting that "vast herds of cattle . . . marked with the owner's initials" roamed over the rich Texas prairie, demonstrating that the common Spanish practice of branding was used even in Austin's colony.

There were a number of local cattle markets such as San Antonio, but an even surer sign of ranching as it became known in the latter

Remuda at water hole, Spur range West Texas, 1909.

MC Ranch buckaroos
moving cattle from desert
to fall grazing land
near headquarters at Adel,
OR. "Buckaroo" is
cowboy transliteration of
Spanish "vaquero," now
designates cowpunchers
of Nevada and Oregon
and some neighboring areas
who love Old West
traditions and dress the
part with elaborate
and expensive gear.

part of the nineteenth century is the fact that both Americans and Spaniards drove their cattle overland to market well before the first longhorns were trailed to Dodge City, Kansas. By 1831 Texans were taking their livestock to Louisiana, selling at ports along the Red and Mississippi rivers and at New Orleans. One rancher near Galveston drove more than 1,000 head to New Orleans in 1834 and sold them at a profit of almost $3 per head.

Finally, both Mexicans and Americans raised the long-horn cow, which became the staple of the Texas ranching industry. A mixed breed combining the more durable characteristics of Spanish and American cattle, the longhorn did not reach his prime until the long trail drives from Texas to the midwestern railheads had tempered and hardened him. But one of Austin's colonists bred a steer in the early 1830s whose horns measured nearly four feet from tip to tip, thus qualifying him as a genuine longhorn.

When the Civil War ended in 1865, the economy of Texas had been ruined. Although wars usually increase the demand for beef, Texas was cut off from the rest of the Confederacy early in the war and was unable to ship its beef to the soldiers. In short, the state was "beef poor." Cattle had been allowed to run wild for five years with virtually no sales. Little organized branding had been done, because the men were away at war. By the time soldiers like twenty-nine-year-old Charles Goodnight returned to their ranches, there were probably three unbranded steers roaming the range for every branded one.

Young Goodnight first decided to leave his Palo Pinto County ranch and seek better employment farther west. "The political condition is sad and gloomy," wrote another future cattle baron, George W. Littlefield. "Our labor is now, or will be, completely demoralized & ruined. No man with the brains of a chicken can entertain the **slightes**[t] **thought** of them improving." Goodnight and hundreds of other cattlemen found that their less scrupulous neighbors had considerably reduced their herds by skillful branding while they were away—from an estimated 5,000 to only 1,000 in Goodnight's case. He was as disgusted as Littlefield with the people, the country, and his chances of establishing a successful ranching operation.

After consideration, however, Goodnight decided to stay in Texas. He first searched for good range land in South Texas, then concluded that it would be easier to use the land he had and drive his cattle to market, rather than to find a new home for the cattle. Many others in Goodnight's position concurred and remained. Littlefield took up cotton farming, but after two failures he turned to trail driving.

Although Texas was economically stagnant at the close of the Civil War, cattlemen realized that money could be made by driving cattle from Texas, where they were bringing $3 to $4 per head, to Kansas City, where they were bringing ten times that amount. The only problem was getting them to market, and both the Mexicans and Texans who had lived and worked cattle in the state prior to the war possessed the ability to trail them to market. The "cow herders" and the vaqueros combined their skills and their cattle. The result was the classic trail drive, the longhorn cow, and the American cowboy.

the trails
and the
towns

At the end of the Civil War, the thousands of men who returned to Texas found millions of cattle running free and unbranded, and all but worthless unless they could be sold to satisfy the new and increasing national taste for beef. Selling meant the new railroad towns of Kansas and Missouri, where steers were worth ten times more than they were in depressed and cash-poor Texas. Ranchers and unemployed trail riders did not take long to decide that their economic salvation lay in walking their stock north to market.

Livestock trail drivers did not originate in the Southwest. They can be traced to colonial America early in the eighteenth century, when Boston, Philadelphia, and Charleston were market centers for drovers. Ohio and Kentucky possessed flourishing ranches while the Texas cattle industry was still in its infancy, and Illinois cattlemen drove herds to market as far away as Boston.

But if most of the nation was unaware of the ranchers of Texas in 1866, Texans themselves were conscious of their identity and confident of their skills. The same men who had wrenched their independence from Mexico in 1836 and endured ten years of haphazard existence as a republic had now survived an even more tragic Civil War and were returning to a style of ranching that was soon recognized as distinctively Texan. The cowpuncher who over the next thirty years pointed the longhorn herds north was an unique combination of skills, techniques, and spirit that could have developed only on the South Texas range. There two cultures, American and Mexican, clashed, mixed, and hardened under pressure from a third—the Indian. Heirs to both an aristocratic and a pragmatic tradition, the Texans seemed natural-born leaders, infusing the same energetic intelligence that is memorialized at San Jacinto and the Alamo into the cattle trade. A Galveston Bay rancher, for example, trailed his herd of cattle eastward over the little-publicized Opelousas Trail to Mississippi early in 1838. That same year some ambitious ranchers in South Texas herded several hundred cattle from the Nueces River to "the interior." Perhaps it was then that wise cattlemen understood what the future economy of the state would be.

Probably the most important element missing from the cattle trade of the 1850s—the element that prevented it from becoming a nationally significant business—was the daring entrepreneurship that marked other successful ventures of the nineteenth century: trapping for furs, steamboating, railroading. That same pioneering spirit characterized the Texans who herded their stock to California a few years after gold was discovered there. Thousands of emigrants rushed to the mines, leaving ranches unmanned, stores untended, and shortages in almost every occupation. Prices skyrocketed: food, clothing, tools. Those who did not enter the goldfields tried to make their fortune selling to the miner.

When cattle-owning Texans realized that their herds might be welcome in California, the kind of organization and leadership that promised development of a significant economic force began. T. J. Trimmier of Washington County, Texas, walked 500 beeves to California in 1848,

Opening pages: Cowboys congregate at Jersey Lilly Bar & Cafe at Ingomar, MT, occasional shipping point and one of last cow towns, with dirt streets, boardwalks, and hitching post. Following pages: Padlock cowboys bringing in a late evening gather for branding.

where he sold them for $100 each. Dozens of drovers were soon on the 1,500-mile trail to California, a considerable distance further than the later, more famous Western, Shawnee, and Chisholm trails that led from Texas to Kansas and Missouri. The California drovers are a relatively unknown part of history, but two cattlemen who left the South Texas region in 1854 kept excellent records. Michael H. Erskine and John James departed within weeks of each other with large herds of Texas longhorns for the Los Angeles market. They arrived in November, taking approximately three months longer than it later took drovers to herd cattle from Texas.

Neither outfit had a difficult time of it, indicating that most of the trail drivers and ranchers probably would have been as successful if they had tried. The work was hard, but the adventure of the trail, the imagined freedom of the cowboy life, and the lure of California attracted hundreds of youths who annually sought jobs with the trail crews. The stories of Indian attacks, vast deserts without water, killing stampedes, and hard work, while true, were not so common as one might believe after devouring cowboy literature or sitting through any of the dozen or so classic films of the last three decades. Otherwise the cowboys would hardly have survived even to work another season, much less to pen their nostalgic memoirs years later.

Many experiences on the California Trail were similar to the events on the later, more famous drives on the Chisholm Trail. The cattle tended to stampede early in the drive, because they had not yet been trail broken. Cowboys went to sleep and allowed cattle to escape, something that most herders did not want to own up to, and something that the code of the trail did not require them to admit, since it was a common and embarrassing occurrence. If possible, they blamed a coyote, an Indian, or a kangaroo rat, which James G. Bell, a member of the James outfit, thought would be delicious if properly cooked. Both Erskine and James reported numerous Indian threats, but never a direct attack. They resorted to night drives while in the desert to avoid the heat, and had trouble pushing the cattle through the mountains. Finally, they both took their cattle over a trail considerably rougher than those that the later drovers used to get to Kansas and Missouri.

The trail leading west out of Texas in 1854 had been open only a few years. The route from Santa Fe to San Diego had been blazed in 1846, when the Americans seized California and the Southwest from Mexico. Two years later a concentrated effort to finish a transcontinental road focused on the Big Bend region between El Paso and San Antonio, the only portion of the trail still unexplored. Merchants sponsored an expedition into this country in 1848 which was almost lost in the desert on the south side of the Rio Grande. The Topographical Engineers fared better, opening the road between San Antonio and El Paso to the mail in 1852. Still it was a difficult route. Later travelers would not wonder at the quality of the road, remarked one of the engineers, but that such a road existed at all. This was the route the drovers took to California.

Erskine left Seguin, Texas, with 942 cattle, 814 of which survived to California. He had heard so many stories of Indian attacks that he employed James H. Callahan, a sometime-Texas Ranger and Indian fighter,

to protect his expedition. On July 4, a day when the rest of America was celebrating the nation's birth and just a few miles away in the neighboring cow camp James Bell was thinking of the "fatherly and philosophical looking face" of Benjamin Franklin "as he stood in Congress hall at the signing of the declaration," Erskine feared Indians were watching his every movement. He knew that red men had attacked one of the earlier trains, killing six or eight men and stealing several cattle. And he knew for a fact that Indians were in the vicinity, because he had entertained a party of Apaches in his own camp and had given them a beef, only to be assured that "all the tribes west of the Rio Grande were friendly."

Erskine probably knew that his drive through West Texas coincided with the "season of the Comanche moon," when Comanches from as far north as Oklahoma rode down the "Great Comanche War Trail" through the Big Bend en route to raids in northern Mexico. The Comanche Trail crossed the drovers' path near Wild Rose Pass, the "most dangerous on the rout," according to Bell, who saw it as the herd passed near the point where Fort Davis was being constructed to protect the western road. When Erskine discovered several oxen missing, he was certain that the Indians had stolen them and dispatched Callahan to recover them. Then he warned nearby trains to be prepared for Indians, but the warnings had little effect, since the trail bosses constantly received rumors from all directions. Callahan trapped the raiders in a canyon where he managed to kill most of them and recovered approximately sixty head of stock that had been stolen from the **haciendas** of northern Mexico. When they reached El Paso the drovers had cleared the most dangerous portion of the trip.

The James outfit did not have as much trouble as Erskine's, perhaps because the first herd acted as a buffer. James' crew had to drink from the tepid water pools stirred up and polluted by Erskine's cattle, but that was a common problem when the trail was so crowded. The picture of life on the James drive is better because Bell, a tenderfoot from San Antonio, was wide-eyed and anxious to note everything in his diary. When the Mexican vaqueros killed a beef, the twenty-two-year-old Bell was astonished to "see with what dispatch 3 Mexicans can rope, kill, and have a beef cut into ropes." The entire party enjoyed the results of the Mexicans' work. "The boys roasted their sun cured meat on the [cow] chips with all the sang froid of Digger Indians," he recorded.

The remarkably consistent climate of the Southwest makes for good cattle country, yet bad weather bothers cowboys and cattle alike. In rain Bell could roll up "in a ball like a porcupine" with his gum coat spread over him, but the cattle had less protection. "About four o'clock in the afternoon a severe rain and Thunder storm came up," he recalled. "The cattle were feeding in the hollow [when] a vivid flash of lightning which made a report like the explosion of [a] thousand cannon, struck a **white** steer, glancing along the belly, and scorching the hair off, thence to another **white** steer—he showed no marks—about fifty yards distant and killed them both, nocking down all—some twenty—intervening and on the line of the stroke." Such incidents only increased the cowboys' fear of lightning storms beyond their superstitions. Teddy Blue Abbott told of one puncher so fearful of lightning that he threw away his revolver so it would not attract a "spark."

Although the cowboys left San Antonio properly attired for and thinking of, no doubt, the saloons of San Francisco, they practiced more utilitarian habits en route. During the first week of the trip the curious Bell saw one of his comrades cutting up three rattlesnakes. Upon inquiry, he found that the fellow intended to put them on his saddle and in his hat. "He told me that by stretching the skin on the cantle of the saddle no harm would come to my posteriors . . . also by putting a pieice of the skin between the

Texas cattle crossing a stream,
from **Harper's Weekly**, 1867.

57

Open-range branding on Benny Binion Ranch, Jordan, MT. Below left: Flanker sits on calf (also "headed & heeled" by two mounted ropers not in picture) as brander approaches. Branding calf (r) and mature Scottish Highlander cow which had escaped earlier branding.

lining and hat, that I never could have the headache." Bell apparently was convinced, because he took part of the skin for his own saddle and hat, but did not comment on its merit.

When he discarded a pair of worn-out pants, Bell was surprised to see that another of his companions picked them up and cut them into sections to make a skull cap. Bell himself soon searched for more practical solutions to his everyday problems. "My riding outfit consists of—on either side of the horn is a **rope** and canteen, behind the cantle is my tin cup and iron spoon, while occasionally there is to be found a dead rabbit hung by the neck waiting to be devoured. And when we expect to travel over dinner time, a slab of jerked beef finds itself flapping against the side of the mule," he wrote.

Clearly this was not the average trail drive that was to become part of American folklore, for diarist Bell was riding a mule. If that does not convince the skeptical, Bell entered another unusual event in his diary: "I had a cup of Tea a few days ago! What do you think of that?" Needless to say what the cowboys around him thought of it.

In a drive that endured for almost six months, Bell had time to consider other facets of life, too. When a Baptist minister traveling with another outfit offered to deliver them a sermon, Bell saw the need for it. The monotony of the trail had rendered most men unable to tell which day was Sunday, but "we are not particularly in need of spiritual food," he reasoned. They were simply bored. "I could sit down and listen with patience to the greatest **ass** who had ever been **called.**"

Amid rumors of Indians and difficulties of the trail, Bell admired the composure of trail boss James. Even in the face of financial loss, James remained unperturbed. "He seemed very cool when informed of the loss of 75 head of cattle," observed Bell, even though the loss occurred because "the guard went to sleep, and the cattle broke for the nearest water." The threat of Indian attack became more real to the drovers when they found the bodies of four of their predecessors under a pile of rocks, but James kept his calm. He ordered that a gunshot be the Indian alarm and intensified his guard.

Bell was one of the many drovers thankful for the scenic West. "The evening is cool and pleasant," he wrote after a tiring day of riding. "The quiet which reigns around would be almost insufferable if it were not for the fine landscape and sunset." "I feel very well this evening," he noted on another occasion, "about as well as could be expected of a man who is on this trip for it is rough and no mistake." Finally, his months on the trail permitted a conclusion: "This is going to California with a vengeance."

Drives to California were highly speculative because they required such a long time, and the cattlemen had no accurate knowledge of the market before they left. But cattle worth $5 to $15 each in Texas were usually priced at $25 to $150 each on the West Coast. That was enough increase in the normal profit for a few adventurous cattlemen to head west every month during the trail-drive season in hopes of improving their profit by selling in the better market.

Despite the lures of California, more conservative Texans

Scant flow of water through wide riverbed. 1901-10.

sought markets for their stock nearer to home. East Texans had long enjoyed a profitable commercial relationship with Louisiana. Short drives reached the river ports in Louisiana or the Texas Gulf Coast. Small paddle boats carried livestock through the choppy Gulf waters as early as 1848, and from 1850 to 1856 Galveston shippers alone accounted for from 3,000 to 6,000 animals annually. Central Texans trailed their cattle to Alexandria, where they shipped them down the Red River to New Orleans. In 1855 Able H. ("Shanghai") Pierce, who later became one of the better-known and more colorful ranchers, participated in his first drive from South Texas to New Orleans. In Texas only a year, the twenty-year-old Pierce went to work for $22.50 a month at the task of getting his Tres Palacios Ranch cattle to the Crescent City.

But the cowboy's reputation—and the rancher's fortune—was made with the northern trail drives to Missouri, Kansas, Wyoming, and Montana. By 1850 such drives were plodding through a youthful Dallas, en route to the shanty towns of the Midwest, where the railroad had momentarily stopped in its transcontinental rush. The Dallas **Herald** editor reported that "several droves of cattle have passed through this place en route to Missouri," where they would either go to furnish teams for emigrants headed for California, or would be shipped to slaughterhouses further north. These drovers were following the old Indian and buffalo trail that pioneers had used to enter Texas. It was soon called the Shawnee Trail, although it had gone by less romantic names early in its history: the Kansas Trail, the cattle trail, or just "trail." The Shawnee Trail led from Austin to Waco to Dallas, then crossed the Red River near Preston, in Grayson County, before striking out for Sedalia or Kansas City, Missouri. The **Texas State Gazette** in Austin reported that some 50,000 cattle left the state via the Shawnee Trail in 1854. It was not called the Shawnee Trail in print until 1874, some twenty years after it had been recognized as an important route.

Trouble threatened the newly developing cattle trade and ultimately helped stop the northern trail drives. As early as 1853 Texans en route to Missouri with their herds had been stopped by indignant citizens who protested the entry of longhorns into their country because they feared Texas fever, a disease carried by ticks. No one knew the cause of the disease in

Evidently caught away from chuck wagon, four Circle Ranch (TX) cowboys prepare a meal on the range. 1901-10.

1853, and the Texans protested for years that they were not responsible for the death and sickness of midwestern cattle. After all, they reasoned, their own cattle were not sick. The fact is that Texas and southern cattle were immune to the fever that caused the stricken animals to arch their backs, droop their heads and ears, and assume other improbable poses. Other symptoms were glassy eyes and a blind stagger. Some even became delirious and broke their horns against trees or the sides of dwellings. Little wonder that the irate midwesterners protested the coming of thousands of infected but immune beasts that sometimes flattened their fences and crops in a stampede, even when behaving normally.

Despite numerous complaints—and some outright interference from vigilantes—the Texans continued to bring their cattle up the Shawnee Trail. Captain Shapley P. Ross bought a herd in Texas at $13 per head and sold it for $27 per head in 1854, making the kind of money that kept the Texans coming. Some drove their cattle farther. Six hundred "fine looking cattle, remarkable for their sleek appearance and long horns" reached Chicago in 1854, and the first Texas cattle reached New York City that same year. Tom Candy Ponting and Washington Malone went to Texas and gathered 700 head of longhorns. They wintered them in Illinois to put on a little fat, then chose 150 of the best ones for the New York market. Shipping them at a cost of $17 each, Ponting and Malone hoped that the Texas longhorn would provide New York diners with a new, low-cost source of beef. But they were disappointed. The cattle tasted something like venison, observed the writer for the **Tribune,** but were "apt to be a little tough when cooked in the ordinary way." Most gourmets would probably disagree, pointing out that the longhorn was tough no matter how he was cooked. The writer for the fledgling New York **Times** was even less complimentary, disdainfully reporting after a first-hand look in 1858 that the cattle "were barely able to cast a shadow." Some other observers probably thought that the "long-legged" cattle with "long taper horns and something of a wild look" might be more at home in the zoo than in a good restaurant. Not surprisingly, New Yorkers did not consume large numbers of longhorns. The number shipped increased slightly from 1856 to 1859, but decreased to less than 100 in 1860, and was cut off completely

cattle trails of the old west

▬▬▬▬▬▬▬	GOODNIGHT-LOVING TRAIL
▬▬▬▬▬▬▬	WESTERN TRAIL
▬▬▬▬▬▬▬	CHISHOLM TRAIL
▬▬▬▬▬▬▬	SHAWNEE TRAIL
▬▬▬▬▬▬▬	CALIFORNIA TRAIL
▬▬▬▬▬▬▬	PROPOSED NATIONAL CATTLE TRAIL

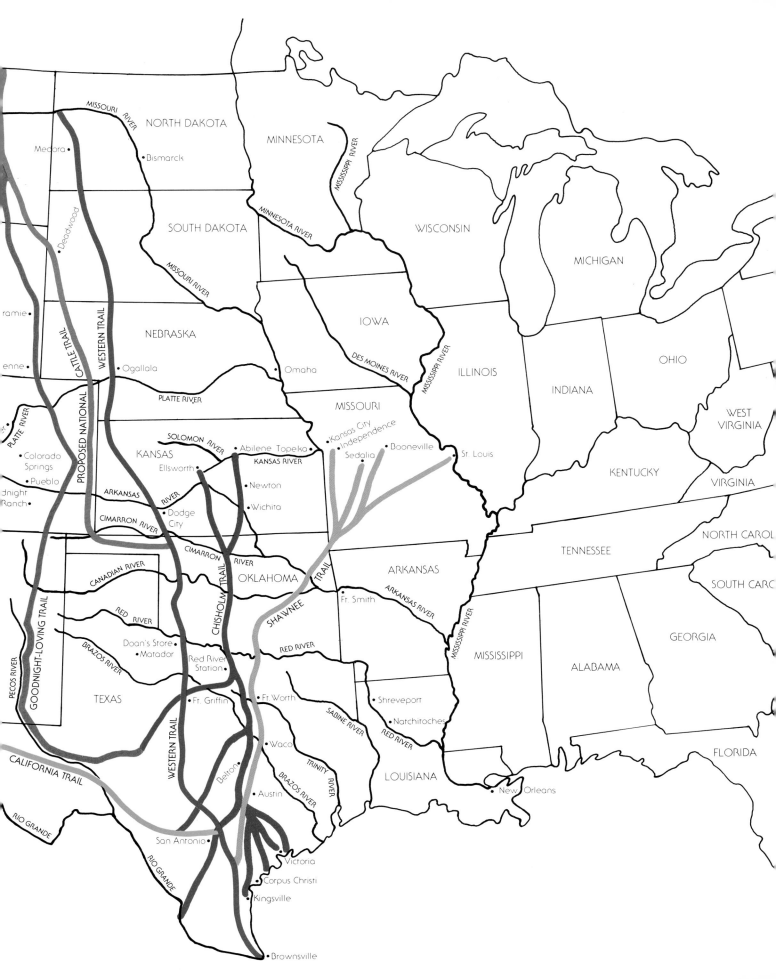

Preceding pages: Spring
roundup wagon crews
of Quien Sabe (top) and
6666's (bottom l). Right:
Moving cattle into
pens for branding.
Cattle have been gathered
over wide area, are
now concentrated near pens,
so Sixes cowboys are
riding close together.

during the Civil War.

The Civil War cut short the expanding Texas cattle trade. Businessmen who had realized the possibilities of the market now turned their efforts to war. Most of the cattle were turned loose while the owners joined the army. But some cattlemen stayed home to provide beef for the Confederacy. Oliver Loving drove cattle across the Mississippi River to the army. When the river was captured by Union forces, thus cutting Texas off from the rest of the South, Texas cattle again ran wild, just as they had under the Spaniards and Mexicans. Some were shipped to Mexico, where they were traded for sugar, powder, cloth, and other scarce items. W. A. Peril drove a herd through the rugged Big Bend country into Mexico in 1864, and Richard King, one of the only ranchers who stayed on his South Texas spread after the Yankees had captured Brownsville and Galveston, engaged in a profitable exchange of cotton and cattle with the Mexican Republic.

Seasoned cowmen knew that the prewar cattle trade had been disrupted by the war. But they also knew that the seeds of potential problems had sprouted before the war broke out. Indians had become more desperate along the western trails, as their homelands gradually decreased and their food supply was killed off by the white man. Americans were taking over their traditional grounds. And the quarantine laws of Missouri and Kansas were being made stricter. In fact, the state legislatures had strengthened the quarantine laws in 1860, during the peak of the cattle trade. So cattlemen returned to their ranches after the war aware of the opportunities that existed, but realizing that something inventive would be required to by-pass the problems looming on the western horizon.

Charles Goodnight was one of the first Texas ranchers released from his army duty. The thirty-year-old cattleman left the Ranger service in 1864 and reentered the cattle business with Charlie Neuhous, getting quite a head start on those cattlemen who did not get out of the army until the following year. Goodnight was unable to take advantage of his early start, however, when Indians disrupted the 1865 drive he had planned for New Mexico and Colorado, and stampeded the cattle. Neuhous salvaged a little profit by herding the remaining cattle to New Orleans. Captain R. H. Williams found a similar situation on his Southwest Texas ranch. The Mexican vaqueros there were living "after the manner of their kind," which to Captain Williams meant that his ranch had not been cared for. "Having no one to look after them, these gentry . . . had been taking things easy," he said, "and everything had been neglected. Calves had been left unbranded and horses allowed to stray away on the prairie." "Every man on this cow hunt was a cattle owner just home from the war and . . . out to see what he had left to brand," said Lee Moore, himself a veteran and a cowboy.

Such negligence had cost Goodnight more than eighty percent of his herd. Using money Neuhous had gotten in New Orleans, the pair rounded up their cattle in 1866, but found only about 1,000 head. The others had been stolen by his neighbors and the Indians. Goodnight felt that most Texans would go north and fight the farmers about the quarantine laws, so he decided to head west to Colorado, where Loving had enjoyed such success prior to the war. Guessing that the western miners had more money to spend on beef than the midwesterners, Goodnight decided to rely upon the experience he had gained as a Ranger to blaze a trail through the western part of the state. If they did not, he knew he could graze his cattle for one year on the rich grassland and sell them the next. Goodnight was doubly fortunate when he met Oliver Loving near Weatherford, Texas, as he prepared for the trek. After hearing of the difficulties of the trail from Loving, Goodnight said he was still determined to go. Since Loving had planned a western drive anyway, he said he would join Goodnight, thus forming a brief partnership that is commemorated by the Goodnight-Loving Trail, traversed by thousands of trail drivers since.

Young Goodnight and the fifty-four-year-old Loving left for Colorado on June 6, 1866. They traveled the route of the Topographical Engineers until they crossed the Pecos River, then they cut northward through New Mexico to Colorado. Other drovers followed their tracks. Captain Williams marched his cattle across part of the Goodnight-Loving Trail before turning south to Mexico. G. T. Reynolds and several others drove their herds along the Concho River to the Pecos, then cut northward into New Mexico. The Goodnight-Loving Trail was soon in constant use.

Correct in their assumption that cattle were worth more money outside Texas, cattle raisers tried other trails to success. H. M. Childress took a herd to Iowa which sold for $35 per head. Monroe Choate and B. A. Borroum followed with 800 steers. E. M. ("Bud") Daggett of Fort Worth trailed his cattle to Shreveport, Louisiana, in 1865, and K. M. Van Zandt hoped that the farmers of the Mississippi Valley would pay a premium price for good Texas beef in 1866. Purchasing 300 cattle on a speculative basis, Van Zandt sent them to the farming regions along the Mississippi, but found that there was no market. Arranging for a Chicago firm to pack the meat in barrels in exchange for the hides, he sold the beef on his next trip to New York. "I had come out about even," he noted in his journal.

Van Zandt was also responsible for one of the more unusual episodes in the history of Nashville's streetcars. He shipped some of his longhorns to Tennessee during an epidemic of what he called the "epizootic"

Drag riders for Matadors trailing a herd from roundup to railroad. 1908.

Opposite: Gary Morton's buckaroo-type gear includes big hat, silk neck scarf, 19-inch boot tops, tucked-in Levis, exaggeratedly high heels. Pistol is for scaring cattle out of brush, killing snakes, security for sole overseer of 60,000-acre line camp for Bells. Below: Bell remuda in rope corral.

Spur cowboys (l) celebrating at Lubbock railroad yard after delivering cattle. Right: Loading longhorns on Central Pacific Railroad at Halleck, UT, 1877.

that killed numerous horses, and some of his longhorns were employed to pull the city's streetcars. Van Zandt was unable to earn enough money to keep him interested in the cattle trade, so he turned with more success to banking. His dabble with cattle gave him enough expertise to enter with some assurance into the booming cattle market in Fort Worth a few years later.

Van Zandt conceded what most drovers already knew: that the real market lay to the north—Kansas and Missouri, where the railroad could ship the steers to feeding grounds or to ready market, but he did not want to battle the quarantine laws that perplexed other cattlemen. At first the Texans tried the direct approach. Colonel John J. Myers confronted the authorities in Missouri, finally managing to sell his cattle at a profit. R. D. Hunter drove his beeves toward Sedalia, where he had more trouble. Halted by a sheriff sporting a coonskin cap, Hunter found himself under arrest. Being a Scot, he did not want to lose the herd, so he convinced the sheriff to take him to a nearby town so a friend could post his bond. When they arrived, Hunter figured the neighborly thing to do was to offer the sheriff a drink. One followed another until Hunter finally left the lawman "blubbering and wallowing in the street." Meanwhile, Hunter's cowboys had moved the herd beyond the sheriff's legal grasp. Hunter drove his cattle through Kansas, then turned eastward to Missouri, where he sold them at a $6,000 profit.

Still, these were not the circumstances of a profitable business. Cattle trails led in three directions from Texas in 1867, but the most profitable one, and the largest market, clearly lay to the north. The problem was that there seemed no way to clear the trails of the legal haze preventing the cattlemen from making full use of them.

Although the quarantine laws prevented Texas cattle from being brought into certain parts of Kansas, the Kansans had not intended to disrupt the trade completely. Trying to please both the farmers and the merchants, the state legislature had left part of the state open to the Texas beef, hoping that the Texas fever would be limited to the less settled portions of the country. Several Kansans acted with more direction. The Topeka Live Stock Company conceived a plan, the outline of which was good, and issued a circular in 1867 inviting the drovers to bring their cattle up an unspecified trail to a soon-to-be-designated depot on the Union Pacific. But there the Topekans faltered. The plan was not firmed up or well publicized.

In Joseph G. McCoy the cattle trade finally got an able businessman willing to promote the industry. McCoy understood both sides of the problem, and presented both the Texans and the Kansans a more interesting package. One of three brothers, McCoy was a slender, unpretentious fellow with a thorough knowledge of the cattle business. His brother

James operated a large farm in Illinois, where the McCoys ran their own cattle and fed those intended for market. William, the third brother, lived in New York City, where he marketed the stock. The McCoy brothers hoped to make money on their scheme, but Joseph had a delicate three-way negotiating problem when he arrived in Kansas in 1867.

He had to deal with the Kansans, the Texas cattlemen, and the railroad. He first visited with officials in several Kansas towns and found that not all residents of the state wanted to keep Texas cattle out. He selected Abilene as the base of his operation. It had the advantage of being on an already established trail and a railroad depot. "The country was entirely unsettled," he said, "well watered, excellent grass, and nearly the entire area of the country was adapted to holding cattle. And it was the farthest point east at which a good depot for cattle business could have been made." Since Abilene lay within the quarantined section of Kansas, he paid a visit to Governor Samuel J. Crawford and wangled a "semi-official" endorsement of his plan. He later got the governor's approval on a map showing how the cattle would reach Abilene. As McCoy returned to Abilene and purchased 250 acres of land outside the city, he knew he had yet to deal with the other faction in Kansas—the aroused local population that would protest the arrival of the first Texas cattle.

McCoy was not the first to think of setting aside a designated railhead where Texas cattle could be brought, but he was the first to promote his plan into reality. The Topeka group never progressed beyond planning. McCoy already had assurances from the Union Pacific Railroad that it would pay him $5 for every carload of cattle he shipped from Abilene, for the railroad had tired of returning its cars to eastern terminals empty. McCoy soon got construction underway on a barn, an office building, a hotel, livery stables, and a bank. He moved in a large set of scales so no one would have to depend upon the traditional range method of "averaging out" the weight of cattle—guessing at their weight.

Having settled the matter with the railroad and the state, McCoy then sent an agent deep into Indian Territory to open negotiations with the third faction, the Texans. At first the cattlemen were suspicious. Having been treated to border ruffians who stole their cattle and beat up the hands, to Indians who either ran off their stock or extracted a fee for the crossing of their land, the Texans could hardly be blamed for their apprehension. Still they had little choice but to accept his offer. They knew of the problems of the previous year in Missouri, so they headed their stock toward McCoy's as-yet-unbuilt pens in Abilene.

The first herd arrived before McCoy finished construction of his pens or hotel. It belonged to Smith, McCord, and Chandler, a northern firm that had purchased the cattle from Texas drovers in Indian Territory. The first herd to forge the new trail under one ownership belonged to Colonel O. W. Wheeler, of California, who had gone to San Antonio with the idea of buying 2,400 steers and driving them to California. But after meeting McCoy's agent, Wheeler turned his herd to Abilene.

A momentary crisis arose when local citizens wrote Gov-

Greene Cattle Co. office at Hereford, AR. 1909. Company still exists.

ernor Crawford protesting that Abilene was in the quarantined zone and that Texas cattle could not legally be driven there, but McCoy had laid his plan carefully, and he solved the problem without further involving the governor. "If I mistake not," wrote Will Lamb of nearby Detroit, "there is a State Law prohibiting any person or persons driving Texas cattle inside the limits of civilization on the frontier: If there is such a law why not enforce it; for there is now, and will be still coming, several thousand head of Texas Cattle in this immediate vicinity." While the governor dallied with the question in Topeka, McCoy held a meeting in Abilene with the irate citizens. While Texas cowboys walked through the group contracting for butter and eggs at increased prices, McCoy promised to pay for all the damages, including dead cattle, caused by Texas fever. The farmers' spokesman seemed convinced by McCoy's offer, and announced, "If I can make any money out of this cattle trade I am not afraid of Spanish fever, but if I can't make any money out of this cattle trade then I am damned 'fraid of Spanish fever."

Despite his efforts, McCoy made little money in 1867 because he started too late in the season. Only the last few herds up the trail went to Abilene, amounting to about 35,000 head, of which fewer than 20,000 were shipped from his pens. But the trend was established, and he shrewdly realized it. The blow-out on the night of September 5, when the first shipment left Abilene, was held in a tent in lieu of the new, unfinished hotel.

McCoy realized that for Abilene to become a cow-town metropolis, a new trail was needed. The Shawnee Trail, over which more than a quarter of a million head of cattle had been walked the previous year, was too far east. McCoy promoted a trail that had been in use for several years, but was largely unused by the drovers. Known to buffaloes, Indians, a few pioneers, and army troops, it was located about 150 miles west of the Shawnee Trail. Major Enoch Steen had marched his six companies of Second Dragoons from Fort Belknap, Texas, to Fort Riley, Kansas, on the trail in 1855. Other soldiers followed in 1861, and by 1864 Indians were using it regularly.

McCoy's trail is perhaps the best-known route of the cattleman's era. It became known as the Chisholm Trail, named for Jesse Chisholm, a half-breed Cherokee Indian who was living with the Wichita Indians in the fall of 1864. A veteran trader and guide born in Tennessee near the turn of the nineteenth century, Chisholm drove wagons up the trail from his trading post near the mouth of the Little Arkansas River to Fort Leavenworth, Kansas, becoming so identified with the trail that others soon called it by his name.

The Chisholm Trail had gone by other names—the Kansas Trail, the Abilene Trail, the McCoy Trail, or simply the cattle trail—but by the time Jesse Chisholm died in 1868, it was commonly referred to by the more famous name. The name first appeared in print in the May, 1870, Eldorado **Daily Commonwealth.**

Combined with other trails, the Chisholm Trail stretched from the southern tip of Texas to Abilene. It ran past the ranching empire of Richard King, past Gonzales, to the state capital at Austin. There it crossed the Colorado River, proceeded to Round Rock (near where the outlaw Sam Bass was killed not long after he helped drive a herd of cattle up the trail), Georgetown, Belton, Comanche Springs, and Fort Worth, itself on the verge of becoming a booming cattle town. The trail crossed the West Fork of the Trinity River there, then continued to Red River Station, which lay on the direct line through Indian Territory to Abilene. It was a more direct route, McCoy advised the Texans. "It has more prairie, less timber, more small streams and fewer large ones, altogether better grass and fewer flies—no civilized Indian tax or wild Indian disturbances—than any other route yet driven over. It is also much shorter because [it is] direct from the Red River to Kansas."

McCoy's promotion was quite a success. More than 50,000 head of cattle arrived in Abilene during 1868, leading the board of directors of the Union Pacific Railroad, usually a cautious bunch, to predict a very large increase in business. McCoy faced a claim of $4,500 from the Abilene area residents for damage caused by the Texas stock during his first year of operation, but he convinced the cattlemen to pay $1,200 of the total.

Soon there were problems that even he could not overcome. Wichita, a cow town further south on the Chisholm Trail, cut into Abilene's business, even though it also was located in the quarantined district. Residents became increasingly vocal in their denunciation of the tick-bearing longhorns. When the Kansas Pacific Railroad voided its contract with him in 1870, McCoy was forced to declare bankruptcy. By 1876 settlements had so enclosed the trail that it was evident that the cattlemen needed a new route, one farther west that would not be molested by civilization.

Texas longhorns being driven through Dodge City, KS, 1878. Cowboys virtually stampeding cattle is probably artistic license.

Fun & Games: Shooting
pool at Cohagen (MT) bar,
"wagon dance" at end
of fall roundup on 06's,
horseplay at Jersey Lily.
Above: About to leave
beautiful downtown Ingomar.
Cowboys from various
ranches linger for
last exchange of news.

Officials of the Santa Fe Railroad created what was to become the most famous of all cow towns. Moving approximately 175 miles southwest of Abilene, they picked Dodge City, a little-known spot fortunately beyond the quarantines, as their new railhead. Dodge City was within the Osage Reservation, but that posed no problem because a rider attached to the Indian Appropriation Bill of 1871 provided that the laws relating to town sites could be extended onto the Osage land. As the Texans blazed a new trail, railroad officials set to work on new pens. By 1876 the Western Trail was in use. Departing the Chisholm Trail at Belton, in Central Texas, the Western Trail headed north through Fort Griffin in West Texas. It crossed the Red River at Jonathan Doan's store, then proceeded through Indian Territory to Dodge City. By 1877 more cattlemen were using the Western Trail than the Chisholm Trail. Shipments in Wichita dwindled to 4,102 that year, while Dodge City shipped 22,940 carloads of beef. Abilene had suffered even more. By 1871 the stockyards income there had diminished a full fifteen percent, with a similar decrease in community revenues. By the spring of 1873 eighty percent of the buildings in Abilene were vacant, and the business community was begging the Texans to return.

Dodge City proved to be the most famous and the longest-lived of the cattle towns. From the first shipment of beeves, success seemed assured. "The grass is remarkably fine, the water plenty, drinks two for a quarter, and no grangers," boasted a reporter for the Dodge City **Times.** "These facts make Dodge City THE cattle point." Dodge was headquarters for dozens of cattle dealers ready to buy what seemed to be any amount of Texas beef. They mixed with scores of cowboys behaving as if they had a reputation to uphold. But Dodge was not the only boom town on the Western Trail. Fort Griffin also prospered from the cattle trade, just as Fort Worth on the

ZX buckaroos heading
out for early
morning "circle"—roundup—
in high country.

Chisholm Trail had a few years before.

Even in the midst of prosperity, shrewd Texans realized that the move from Abilene and Wichita to Dodge City was only a temporary solution to their problem. The primary cattle trail could not be shifted westward every time civilization threatened to enclose it. They had to search for other answers. Railroads had come to Texas, of course, but it was cheaper and easier to trail a herd to Kansas and ship from there than to ship from Fort Worth or San Antonio. Besides, longhorns, because of their long horns, were difficult to ship, and only a few could be placed in a boxcar. (The later development of shorthorns eased this problem.)

South Texans thought they had the solution as ranchers from across the nation gathered in St. Louis in 1884 for the first national cattlemen's meeting. Foremost among their proposals was a recommendation for a National Trail. They wanted a trail under Federal control (which would therefore override any state legislation) that would extend from South Texas, through Oklahoma, around Kansas (because of the quarantine), through Colorado, Nebraska, South Dakota, Wyoming, and Montana into Canada.

There was considerable support for the resolution, because the Texans themselves made up forty-seven percent of the delegates. But some Kansans favored it, too, because they wanted to see the Texans limited to only one trail.

Texas Senator Richard Coke and Congressman James F. Miller introduced bills in both houses of Congress outlining the proposal for a National Trail in December, 1884. They asked for a trail six miles wide to be laid out by three commissioners chosen for that purpose by the Secretary of the Interior. Coke and Miller envisioned grazing grounds and quarantine grounds, as well as crossings for local cattle at designated points, where the trail would be no more than two hundred feet wide. All the land for the trail would be withdrawn from the public domain and reserved for that purpose for ten years.

The National Trail concept never really had a chance. Texans supported it because they saw it as the answer to their problem. It would have given them an alternative to paying high railroad fees from Texas or combating irate citizens in Kansas. But almost no one else supported the plan. Northerners who had plenty of cattle opposed it because they did not want to have any more competition from the longhorns. Kansans feared Texas fever, so they opposed it. Ranchmen in Wyoming, Dakota, and Montana grazed their cattle on public domain and did not want to share it with cattle from Texas, so they also opposed it.

The northern ranchers might have thrown their support behind the National Trail idea if the Texans had been willing to compromise with them. The northerners wanted legislation permitting the public domain to be leased for grazing. Fearful of being evicted from the grassland at any moment, these ranchers would have welcomed such a law that guaranteed their grazing rights for several years. Thinking that this would have prevented them from grazing their cattle on public domain when they were in northern regions, the Texans would not equivocate, so both measures failed.

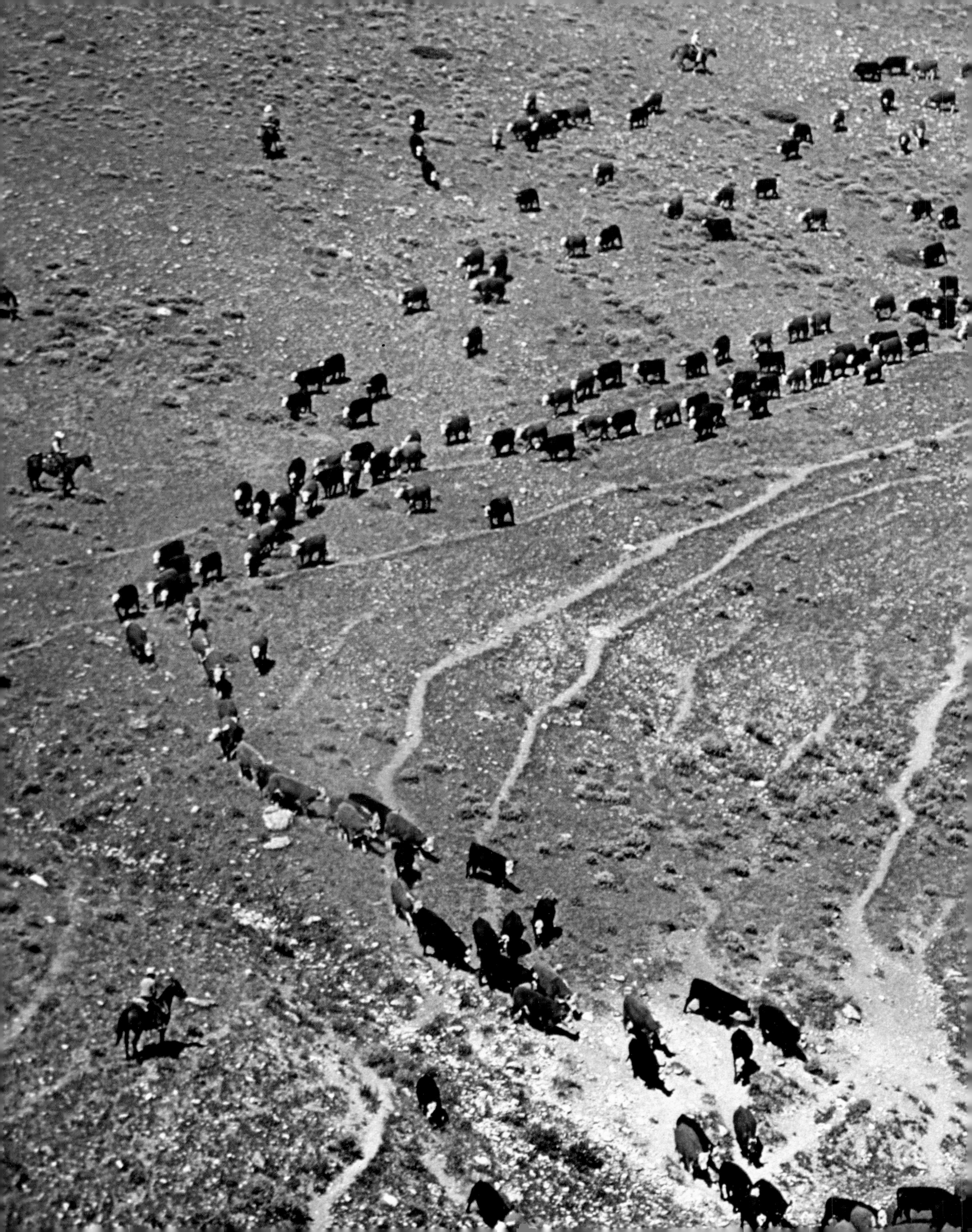

4

the
trail
drive

Except in the way the western cowboy practiced it, the trail drive itself was not unique. His predecessors in Europe and colonial America had driven cattle to market, but the cowboy lived with the cattle, camped out for the three months of the drive from Texas to Kansas, and slept on the ground nightly. He got up before the sun to begin his work and did not turn in until the summer sun had set. In between he stood his turn at watch, losing two or three hours of sleep. Throughout the drive the cowboy ate only the chuck that the cook had on his wagon, which in at least one instance was so mundane that the cook quit rather than serve it. Meanwhile, the day was filled with hard, difficult work, for a herd of 3,000 cattle did not maintain itself. Even so, the cowboy did not lose his pride or sense of humor. There were more than adequate rewards for anyone working for Texan John Blocker, said one cynical hand. You could always count on "two suppers every night. One after dark and the second befo' sunup the next mo'nin'."

Despite the demanding hours and even more demanding job, countless youngsters sacrificed home for the trail. They watched cowboys walk and ride and swore to imitate them. They read dime novels and left for the trail inspired to challenge Texas Jack's or Buffalo Bill's greatest feats. "I became restless and expressed a desire to make a trip up the trail as a cowpuncher," recalled nineteen-year-old Baylis John Fletcher. His maiden-aunt Ellen "remonstrated vigorously against the idea of a mere boy's going up the trail," but Fletcher finally met all her objections and headed north with a local outfit. Andy Adams boasted in his classic novel of the trail that, "By the time I was twenty there was no better cow-hand in the entire country. The vagabond temperament of the range I easily assimilated." "I was a cowhand looking for adventure," concluded W. A. Askew, "and I found it."

The trail drive was not just a character-building school for ambitious wanderers, but was also an original piece of Americana. In many ways it resembled a military expedition, as the boss gathered his crew, rounded up the cattle, and set out for Dodge City, Sheridan, or one of the other small cattle towns that dotted the Kansas Pacific and Union Pacific railroad lines. A sure sign of spring, said the Denver **Field and Farm** newspaper, was when the cowboy donned "his summer sombrero," straddled his "restless bronco," and set out across the plains to the "distant cow-camp to get a job for the season." The Santa Fe **New Mexican** predicted that the spring roundup was near when the cowboys began to stock up on "tobacco, poor whiskey and cartridges." Cowboy Mat Ennis Jones probably had a surer method of forecasting, because he noted that the trail boss always waited until the full spring moon, so the boys who had to stand guard at night would have more light.

The most important member of the crew was the trail boss himself, who was hired first if he were not a regular member of the ranch crew. Old trail bosses were so numerous in Texas that they formed a respected social class and reminisced annually at the publicity-bathed Old Trail Drivers Association meetings in San Antonio long after the last herd had gone up the Chisholm Trail. The trail boss led the herd. He picked among several trails to his destination and watched for the best camping spot. He scouted several miles ahead of the herd to make sure the route was clear of any obstacles. He usually inspired intense loyalty among his men. "A foreman like Johnny was worth an awful lot of money to an outfit," opined Teddy Abbott. "He handled the herd. You've no idea how easy it is to knock a dollar off a beef; your profit all depends on moving them along quiet and easy, and with those wild cattle it took kid gloves . . . . I've never seen a man that handled cattle as smooth as he did, just as smooth as silk, and he handled men the same way. There wasn't a man in his outfit that wouldn't go to hell for him." For all this, Johnny probably received $125 a month.

Often an old cowpuncher who could no longer ride but who longed to stay around cooked for the men. Well worth his $35 to $55 per month, he, if anybody, worked longer hours than the trail boss. Up at 3 a.m. to start the coffee boiling, he enticed the punchers from their sleeping bags with the ubiquitous pancakes and bacon. Breakfast over, he moved out ahead of the herd to help the trail boss find a good spot for dinner (lunch) before the boys reined up for a quick break. He performed the same drill in time for supper, except this camping spot had to accommodate the crew for the night.

By tradition if not by temperament, the cook was a determined cuss with his own set of rights and privileges. He was boss around the chuck wagon, which served as social center, hospital, and wardrobe for the cowboy. The westerner aphorized the cook's special prerogatives with such terse phrases as: "Crossin' a range cook's as risky as braidin' a mule's tail."

Mundane food was the rule of the day. Butter and eggs spoiled on the trail, so corn meal, sorghum molasses, beans, salt, and bacon had to break the monotony of the ever-present beef and coffee. Teddy Blue concluded that one reason so many Texas cowboys stayed in Montana was not because Montana was such better ranch land as much as it was because they could not bear to face the cook's chuck all the way back to Texas.

The chuck wagon was, on the other hand, a compact arrangement, the result of several decades of evolution. When vaqueros and cow herders first started handling cattle from horseback, each man carried his own food in a saddlebag or flour sack. A pack mule soon replaced the saddlebag, but was later hitched to a two-wheeled cart instead. Unfortunately, the two-wheeled cart was too slow to keep up with the cattle on longer drives. Some historians claim that Charles Goodnight invented the chuck wagon that soon covered the Plains. Rather than the wooden carts, Goodnight used wagons with iron axles and greased them with tallow. He added a chuck box to the rear and suggested some later refinements that enabled the cook to load food, water, cow chips (for fuel), a cabinet, and several other necessities of range life on the wagon. Later wagons carried beds for the trail boss and cook, ropes, mesquite stakes and pegs for the horse wrangler's corral, and often a kerosene lantern.

The cowboy rode well, worked hard, ate dust, wrestled cattle, avoided stampedes, and earned $25 to $40 per month plus grub. Most were seasonal workers, hired only for the drive. Sometimes they returned for the next season, but wandering was the inherent right of a puncher who

Preceding pages: Binion wagon outfit in Missouri Brake country of Montana. Two-horse hoodlum wagon (firewood, irons, tarps, odds & ends) leads. Four-horse chuck wagon (stove, water, food) and four-mule bed wagon follow. Cavvy—a regionalism for remuda—of 90-100 horses trails. Opposite: Roy Blackwell, Quien Sabe wagon cook, his kitchen (below), making sourdough biscuits (bottom). Rubber-tired wheels are necessary when wagon is trailered on highway to QS range in Oklahoma.

85

usually moved on to another range. A cowboy lasted only a few years under such trying circumstances. James McCauley had to quit cowboying before he was thirty years old. "For a man to be stove up at thirty may sound strange to some people, but many a cowboy has been so bunged up that he has to quit riding that early in life," said McCauley. "To make a long story short, I have done as most cowpunchers do after they have got too stove up to ride. I went back to my early raising"—which in McCauley's case was farming.

With the addition of a horse wrangler, the roundup crew was complete. In charge of the remuda (as the horse herd was called in the Southwest) or cavvy (in the Northwest) that might contain as many as sixty to 100 horses, the wrangler made sure the horses had the best possible grazing. Mat Jones, himself an old-time cowboy, rated the wrangler, who was sometimes a boy too young to trail-drive but who could tend the horses and keep the equipment, next in importance to the cook in keeping the outfit operating smoothly.

The wrangler usually got up with the cook to put up the rope corral, a rather ingenious device for permitting the men to rope their horses without chasing them all over the range. The horses grazed and slept hobbled each night. Each morning the wrangler put up the corral by sticking pegs into the ground to form a circle and securing them with stake ropes. Then he would stretch a rope from peg to peg, making a corral to hold the horses while the boys roped and saddled them. The rope corral could be put up quickly, taken down quicker, and tossed in with the other equipment.

If the rancher did not want to go to the trouble to put a herd on the trail, he could contract his cattle to a professional cattle trailer or sell them. One of the little-known aspects of ranching concerns the professional men who made their living driving cattle up the well-known trails to market. Most of the ranchers preferred not to drive their cattle to market. They kept their cowboys at home so they could tend to the numerous chores always needing attention on a working ranch. Most of the cowboys who rode and roped their way into the myths and legends of today did it while working for a professional cattle trailer. Some of the best-known barons of the range started their careers driving cattle to market—theirs or others, contracted or purchased: Ike T. Pryor, John T. Lytle, Eugene B. Millet, even Charles Goodnight.

All roundups were basically the same, whether conducted

"Breaking camp," southern Colorado, 1880. A fanciful view, actually incorporating many of cowhands' morning activities.

by the rancher or by a cattle trailer, whether intended for a trail drive or simply for branding the new calves. In the spring cattlemen gathered their livestock off the open range. Theirs would be mixed with other stock, so each rancher in the area sent one or more "reps" to observe and collect his stock. Separating one rancher's cattle from the herd belonged to another soon-developed skill called "cutting." Good saddle horses could be trained for the task, finally becoming so automatic that the cowboy only headed toward the steer and sat back while the horse did the work. In an ideal demonstration, the puncher rides his horse toward the cow, then gives the horse his head. The horse separates the cow from the herd and prevents her from returning while the rider's hands rest casually on the saddle horn.

The self-policing aspects of ranching were most obvious at roundups. If a cowboy accidentally misbranded a calf, the mistake was corrected on the next calf. Should another cattleman's steer be taken to market, it was sold and the money given to the owner after the return home. The process often broke down, however, the famous "MURDER" calf in the Big Bend being the best example. During a Big Bend roundup in 1891, two cowboys disputed the possession of a maverick. One cowboy killed the other, and the remaining punchers branded the calf with neither of their brands but with the word "MURDER" instead. Most historians think that the calf went with the herd to Montana, ending the saga, but legend insists that the brand grew to enormous size and turned red, that the steer's coat turned silver grey, and that he went all over the Big Bend looking in saloon windows trying to find the cowboy who caused him to be so marked.

Still honesty was the primary rule of the range. Ike Pryor remembered that for years after he sent 15,000 head northward in 1884, cattlemen would come up to him at the various cattlemen's conventions and pay him for cattle that had strayed from his herd onto their range. They eventually sold the cattle and wanted to pay him for them. When a large part of the population ceased to be honest, the ranching industry developed many problems, the most bothersome of which, rustling, has not yet been solved.

An 1888 roundup on the Maxwell Land Grant Company ranch near Taos, New Mexico, was typical of the drive preparations. The boys gathered their gear, loaded the chuck wagon, and headed out to a canyon to hunt cattle. Up early the next morning, "everything . . . a bustle," they gulped

their breakfast, the wrangler brought the horses nearer the camp, and each puncher saddled his bronc. As the boys spread out across the country, there ensued a "wild and exciting scene," wrote Leon Noel, a New Yorker spending his summer in the West on doctor's orders. The cattle were not so easy to handle as horses. "On all sides the cattle break away from the main herd, and go tearing back in the direction from whence they came, with the cowboys following in full chase. Up hill, down hill, across the cañon, through brush and water! And such dodging . . . . Why, it's as bad as a flea hunt!"

An 1862 Nevada roundup over worse terrain proved to be less fun. "The object of the expedition," began J. F. Tripplett, who eventually bossed the drive, "is to collect a large band of cattle and to recover, if possible, from the Pah-Ute Indians a number of horses and cattle which were stolen." The riders headed, uncowboylike, into the desert without naming a boss until they had been out for several days. Then they elected captain the largest rancher in their company. "All hands jubilant that they are going to have a good time," wrote Tripplett, "but they don't know the country; Hell is an ice house to some of the places they'll see before a week passes."

The new leader proved notably inept at rounding up cattle, as several citations from Tripplett's diary indicate:

"May 8.—Accomplished nothing.

"May 9.—Worse than yesterday.

"May 10.—Repetition of the ninth.

"May 12.—Only one horse left in camp; balance gone to hunt **cold** water. One man gone to hunt horses. Boys beginning to find that the sun can shine hot. One small wagon for twenty-two men to crawl under to get in shade; no tents, no willows, no sticks to stretch a blanket over, not even sagebrush. Hot, hotter, d--d hot." Tripplett wryly remarked that "every man will sleep with a rope in his hand" tonight.

His cynicism continued on May 13—"don't know why we are up here, unless to keep out of the way of cattle"—but the well-known cowboy humor quickly asserted itself. "There has been a good deal of growling and grumbling among the men, and at my suggestion the company has elected Jim Benson as chief growler. No other man will be allowed to grumble at anything." Finally, the rancher who had been elected captain admitted that he did not know enough about the habits of cattle to find them in such rough country, and the punchers named Tripplett their boss. Several weeks more produced over 1,300 cattle belonging to ranchers in the Carson City area.

Sometimes unscrupulous cowmen sold the same cattle repeatedly. Perhaps that was the goal of Shanghai Pierce as he rounded up cattle in April, 1871, to sell to a Kansas cattle trailer. One of Pierce's hands, Charles A. Siringo, recalled that they were branding up to 400 mavericks a day while working along the headwaters of the Tres Palacious Creek. After a month's work they turned over 1,100 semiwild Texas longhorns to the Kansan and his midwestern cowboys. By the time they reached the Red River, claimed Siringo, they had lost all the cattle and returned to Kansas empty-handed. The would-be cowman returned to his former trade of blacksmithing in Dodge City, where Pierce saw him the following year. He "cursed Texas

shamefully and swore he never would, even if he should live to be as old as Isaac, son of Jacob, dabble in long horns again." Although Siringo did not suggest that Pierce was trying to cheat the Kansan out of the cattle, Pierce would have sold them again if they had drifted back onto his range.

Many range terms, including the word "maverick," come from the South Texas roundups. Maverick is credited to Samuel A. Maverick of San Antonio, a respected resident and rancher. Following the Civil War, all of Maverick's neighbors reportedly branded their cattle, but Maverick chose to leave his unbranded, telling them that since theirs were all branded, they would be able to recognize his by the absence of a brand. Maverick supposedly then claimed all unbranded cattle as his, including those belonging to his neighbors that had not yet been branded. Soon every time someone saw an unbranded calf, they would scoff: "There goes one of Mr. Maverick's cattle," which old-timers pronounced in two syllables as if it were spelled "mavrick."

After the cattle were separated, the Maxwell Land Grant cowboys marked their cattle in the old way: They roped the calves and dragged them, bawling and kicking, to the fire where the branding irons heated. Since calves stayed with their mothers, the hands marked each calf with the mother's brand. One cowboy held the calf down while another applied the iron and another cut the ear to further expedite identification. A third cowboy castrated the animal at the same time

Ready to begin the drive north, the crew used special chutes to apply the road brand. A chute was made of two parallel rows of heavy stakes jammed about two feet into the ground and two tall timbers called the "snapping turtle" standing vertically at the end. Spaced about ten inches apart at the bottom, the stakes spread to four feet at the top, forming a "V." Once the cattle ventured curiously into the chute, they could not turn around. When they reached the two tall timbers at the end, one swung against the other, trapping the steer, and he was branded. The whole operation took only a few seconds. Other crews took more time because they used the traditional method of roping the cattle on the open range and branding them.

The road brand was different from the regular mark of the rancher, usually indicating that the herd had been sold to the drover. The trail boss carried papers proving that the owner of the first brand had legally sold or assigned the cattle to him. Since the brands were all a matter of public record, no one could simply make up a brand for stolen cattle and expect to get away with it.

Although the departure was not accompanied by as much heraldry and pomp as the movies usually depict, the hands were excited as they headed out. The drive climaxed several grueling weeks of roundup and branding, and the cowboys were ready for a change. "On the morning of April 11, a supreme moment for us, we started up the trail to Cheyenne, Wyoming," recalled Baylis John Fletcher. They made only five miles the first day because the cattle did not work easily. And three nights later the cattle stampeded when Fletcher and his partner were lulled into a false sense of security.

Twenty-four-year-old Ben C. Mayes, a Tom Green County cowboy, started his first cattle drive even more slowly. He arrived in camp just as the drive began. The "Boss Says here is hell and we all Scater out and Started the drive all Hollowing and cattle Running in ever direction," recalled Mayes. "I tried to Keep Sight of Some of the Boys But they got out of my Sight and I dident no more know where I was than nothing[.] only I was on the Steak Plains and In Texas I guessed . . . and it was hell for me for I never found camp for three days . . . ." Mayes was embarrassed but glad when two of his companions led him into camp.

Trail drivers routinely expected the herd to stampede and took extra precautions to prevent it early in the drive. Cowmen counted on losing perhaps ten percent of their stock because of stampedes, but the loss often was greater. Cowboys on the Mitchell Ranch in the Big Bend had corralled their cattle in a natural triangle called Robbers Roost. Two sides of the corral were high cliffs, and the third was the rimrock itself. As the cowboys sat around the campfire, an ominous silence fell. Every cowhand recognized the roar that crescendoed around them. The cattle were stampeding! The rock wall held them on one side, but hundreds careened over the precipice on the opposite side before the screaming, blanket-waving cattlemen could calm them. Arthur Mitchell and several men rode to the bottom of the cliff to view the ruins: "mountains of meat—gory from torn flesh. Grotesque shapes with broken necks, broken horns; here and there slight movement indicating that somewhere below were a few not yet smothered. We didn't say much," reflected Mitchell, "for we were all thinking that we might have been carried over the bluff if we had been caught in the run."

Stampedes were easy to start but difficult to stop. A rapid change in the weather, a wolf, a rat, bad water—almost any excuse was adequate to set the high-strung beeves on their destructive path. Sometimes the cowboys could only save their lives. "It occurred during our guard," said a Big Bend cowboy of the most destructive stampede in his career. "Officer's horse suddenly struck a gopher burrow with his front feet, and in a moment horse and rider were sprawling on the ground. . . . The cattle headed toward me . . . and I had to use both quirt and rowell to keep clear of the onrush."

Ingenious cowboys exhausted their resourcefulness with ill-fated plans to prevent stampede, but the longhorn's cantankerous nature

Cowboy roping his mount from remuda within rope corral. Shoe Bar. 1908.

"The Drive," perhaps Erwin Smith's most famous photograph.

Preceding pages: Lunch at QS wagon. Range diet is unvarying: all forms of beef (including son-of-a-bitch stew of indescribable leftovers), beans, canned vegetables, sourdough bread, pie, tea, coffee. Difficulty of finding good wagon cooks is one reason for gradual demise of team-drawn chuck wagons.

won out. The best solution was to tire out the steers with long drives during the first several weeks on the trail. They seemed to drive better after they got used to the routine. Others suggested that songs lulled them into a trance that was hard to interrupt, but Andy Adams believed he offered the sure cure: "Boys, the secret of trailing cattle is never to let your herd know that they are under restraint," he advised. "Let everything that is done be done voluntarily by the cattle. . . . Never let a cow take a step, except in the direction of its destination. In this manner you can loaf away the day, and cover from fifteen to twenty miles, and the herd in the meantime will enjoy all the freedom of an open range."

Adams was right in that the biggest part of handling cattle was technique, but the technique was known and practiced by all and still did not solve the more difficult problems. The accepted procedure called for cowboys to align themselves around the herd in positions called pointers, swing riders, flank riders, and drag riders. The more respected, experienced cowhands rode point to keep the herd from mixing with any other herd and to head off possible stampedes. Point riders commanded the herd while the trail boss was searching ahead for the next camp. Swing riders and flank riders protected the sides of the herd, swinging out, then riding back toward the herd in an action that soon became automatic and enabled them to keep the herd moving at a leisurely pace, while losing few strays.

Following the herd, drag riders caught all the dust of the trail as they headed the stragglers back to the main bunch. "I have seen them come off herd with the dust half an inch deep on their hats and thick as fur in their eyebrows and mustaches," said Teddy Blue, "and if they shook their head or you tapped their cheek it would fall off them in showers." Drag riders usually were young men who were desperate for a job. "The poorest men always worked the drags," said Teddy, "because a good hand wouldn't stand for it." Although a good cowboy would rather quit than ride drag, Teddy Blue felt that the rest of them were pretty nearly as bad off when they were on the side away from the wind. "They would go to the water barrel at the end of the day and rinse their mouths and cough and spit and bring up that black stuff out of their throats. But you couldn't get it up out of your lungs."

Dime novels had not told them of the other hardships of the trail, but most youngsters just starting out soon learned that more than desire was necessary to work a real herd. When Mat Jones' trail boss assigned him a bay, Jones sensed the horse had lots of spirit by the way the other punchers looked at him. Plucky because of what he thought was the boss' confidence in him, Jones started down the trail. "All of a sudden the hounds jumped a rabbit under my horse's nose," he recalled. "That bay threw down his head, and the first jump he made I lit on his neck in front of the saddle. On the next jump the saddle hit my rear end, and I lit on my head against a mesquite tree. I felt as if my neck were broken, and I reached up with both hands to twist it into place."

Jim McCauley hazarded a similar ride coaxing seventy-five surly longhorns back into the main herd. His horse stumbled and rolled over him. "He mashed me some," admitted McCauley. "When he fell he kindly knocked me senseless, as my head hit the ground first. The horse broke a front leg . . . and I could not get my leg out from under him. The St. Louis Cattle Co. was out a good horse and liked to have been out a cowboy," concluded McCauley, who lay under the animal for hours before he finally managed to signal his friends by firing shots into the air.

Natural obstacles plagued the cow hands as they pushed the herd up the trail. The problems are familiar. Portions of the trail were waterless, especially the westward-leading routes. Cowboys knew them well, planned the drive so they spent minimum time without water, and watched the steers more closely because they stampeded more easily when thirsty.

On the other hand, cowboys also dreaded too much water. George C. Duffield, an Iowa cowboy, was caught in an unusually wet spring as he headed a thousand cattle northward. "Raining for three days," he penciled in his damp diary. "These are dark days for me." A few days later: "Rain pouring down in torrents & here we are on the banks of a creek with 10 or 12 ft water & rising." "Still dark and gloomy," he wrote the following day. "River up everything looks **Blue** to me[.] no crossing to day[.] cattle behaved well[.]" The herd stampeded four times during the first two weeks of the drive, and Duffield recovered only about half of them. The weather rendered the roads almost impassable as he reached Red River. "Herd travelled 18 Miles over the worst road I ever saw & come to Boggy Depot & crossed 4 Rivers," he noted. "It is well Known by that name[.]"

Rampaging rivers created special problems for drovers. Cattle feared water and often hesitated to swim. Will Tom Carpenter might have guessed that he would have trouble when he approached the Pecos River with a herd in 1892. The weather was already "trying to storm and do Everything Else but something nice," and he had somehow lost the herd in the thick fog on three different occasions. He first thought the crossing would be easy because the cattle were thirsty and went to the water to get a drink. The Pecos was only about belly-deep on the cattle and a shallow bank waited to welcome them not sixty yards away on the other side. "But we could not get them to lead out," Carpenter exclaimed. "We worked for an hour or so trying to Cross them. We would rope calves and drag them across, and their mothers would follow over after them. And we would tie the calf over there and go back and get another one and do the same way." At one point Carpenter had six calves tied and waiting on the other side of the river, but the herd still balked.

Raised in the mountains near Alpine, Texas, the cattle apparently refused to cross because they had never seen so much water. Perplexed, Carpenter backed the herd up and bedded down for two nights while he tried to outsmart his longhorns. Finally he urged them back to the river and camped for the night. "I told the Boys that If they never did Cross,

that we would have their bones all close together so that the bone haulers [who collected and sold bones of buffalo and other animals] would not have any trouble loading their wagons." Apparently the nearness of the water quelled their fear. The following morning the recalcitrant longhorns waded across the Pecos, and Carpenter finished his drive in three days, less time than it took him to cross the Pecos.

Often the longhorn's fear of water was justified, for if they were not properly handled, death to both cowboy and cow might result. Almost a thousand head of cattle were lost in an 1877 New Mexico drive as a herd of 3,000 approached the Pecos. A correspondent for **Leslie's Illustrated Newspaper** described "the most exciting scene it has been my fortune to witness during a twenty years' experience on the frontiers." The braying of a donkey at dawn set the herd off in the direction of the river, some two miles distant. Experienced cowboys spurred their horses in an effort to keep the cattle from plunging over the fourteen-foot bank. Some were diverted, but when an inexperienced cowboy panicked and stopped his horse in front of the herd, all effort was directed toward saving him. His horse showed more presence of mind by bucking the rider off and running to safety. Another cowboy rode into the path of the herd at the last instant and rescued the stunned puncher.

The bulk of the herd turned, but it was impossible to save those nearest the river. Hundreds lunged into the water, "a solid mass of the beasts," noted the startled correspondent. "Such a Babel of sounds! Such a confusion of sights! More than a thousand cattle were struggling in the river." Those on the bottom were drowned or crushed, and hundreds suffered broken limbs or ribs. More than 800 perished "in less time than it takes to tell it," concluded the amazed reporter. The cowboys rounded up the others and continued the drive.

Cattle-trailer Ike Pryor experienced what surely is one of the most unusual incidents in trail-driving history. Herding cattle up the Arkansas River in 1875, he encountered several men who warned him that a huge buffalo herd ahead would block his route. But Pryor pushed on, confident in his ignorance. Suddenly he saw a giant cloud in front of him and reluctantly concluded that there might have been something to the warning. Then he saw undoubtedly one of the largest herds left on the prairie. "The front of the herd was so wide that neither edge was in sight," he exclaimed. He shot at them. His drovers waved yellow slickers in their faces. Finally the bison split. Pryor watched in bewilderment as the rangy creatures engulfed his frightened herd. "Those buffaloes were passing us all night long," he wailed. "At daylight next morning they were still passing by but the tail end was in sight." Pryor was lucky. He had kept his startled cattle together while for twelve hours the great wave of bison flowed to one side and the other of his herd.

Compared to bison, Indians were a more consistent but usually minor irritation. The Indian Act of 1834 empowered reservation Indians to charge cattlemen $1 per head of cattle driven across their land without their permission, thus establishing the Indians' right to charge a toll. A beef from each herd was the usual payment for grass the cattle ate as they crossed the reservation. But some Indians stopped the drovers several times, as various warriors enriched their own herds. The cattlemen had little choice but to pay, because the alternative was legal action or, more probably, an Indian-inspired stampede.

Unbusinesslike Indians were an even greater problem, as cow hands on the California trail learned. Remembering the inflated prices paid before the Civil War, several drovers set out enthusiastically for the West Coast in 1869. But not many of them made it. According to the San Diego **Union,** only about 4,000 head out of an estimated 55,000 reached California. "One man alone left California to go to Texas after cattle," continued the editor. "He invested all his money in cattle and started with them but arrived in San Diego County without a single head. . . . The Indians were continually stampeding the cattle; and the long trip, bad weather and other casualties left the adventurer cattleless. This is not an isolated case. . . ."

Perhaps the most serious problem the Texans faced was irate citizens in Kansas and Missouri who demanded that the longhorns be kept out of their country because of Texas fever. Initially the Texans were welcome. Some of the early pioneers were so poor, in fact, that they actually invited the drovers to bed their herd down near their house for a couple of nights so they could gather the cow chips for fuel the following winter, but with the onslaught following the Civil War, Texas fever became the dreaded enemy of every Kansas and Missouri stockman. The same onslaught—and increased prices— encouraged Texans to head their cattle north in 1867, but they met farmers and merchants organized to banish the Texas fever menace.

An extreme example of citizen interference prevented J. M. Daugherty from getting his cattle to Sedalia in 1866. A band professing sympathy with Unionist guerrillas of the Civil War attacked Daugherty's cowboys, killing the point man and stampeding the beeves. Daugherty himself was beaten but finally released, probably because he was only sixteen years old. The incident angered drovers all the way to Texas, who rightly suspected the bandits were simply using handy excuses to rob cattlemen.

Shoe Bar cowboys "stringing out" a
herd—keeping it from bunching
—Tongue River, TX, 1905-10.

Preceding pages: Afternoon
circle coming together
for branding on Four Sixes.
Herd will be held in trap
—small fenced pasture—
till morning, making
''nighthawking'' unnecessary.
Opposite: Action on
the MC's during
impressive ten-day March
drive of some 4,000
head over high desert.
Buckaroo at bottom
had just joined MC's from
ORO outfit, Prescott, AR.

Texas fever, however, was a real threat to the livestock of the Midwest, bringing action on the part of state legislatures and local committees. Texans had to reroute their cattle on several occasions. In 1885 the obstruction was so severe that herds backed up on the Western Trail almost to Texas. Early in July the editor of the Fort Worth **Gazette** reported that 25,000 head had been stopped. A few months later the Abilene, Texas, **Taylor County News** reported that the number had increased to more than 100,000.

The trail drive ended in a much-heralded assault upon decency in such towns as Abilene, Kansas. Abilene, a "small, dead place, consisting of about one dozen log huts" when Joseph McCoy first saw it in 1867, was the first of the cattle towns cut from the traditional mold—a town built almost completely on the cattle trade. Others followed: Ellsworth, Caldwell, Wichita, and Dodge City in Kansas; Cheyenne, Wyoming; and Kansas City and Sedalia, Missouri. The Kansas cattle towns have inspired reams of literature, superficial, machismo movies, some pretty fair art, and, today, "Old West" towns as adjuncts to many midwestern cities. In reality, the arrival of the punchers in town is a brief bit of Americana that seems to have been sapped of all its intrinsic interest and embroidered with stories the equal of Parson Weems' fable of George Washington and the cherry tree. The stereotypical movie scene in which the cowboy strides into the no man's land of the saloon to down a drink, the inept marshal warns the trail boss to take his ruffians outside town, or the punchers shoot up the main street and return the following day to pay for the saloon's shattered gilt-edged mirror, serve to prove that in many instances fiction is more interesting than truth.

When drovers approached town, the trail boss or owner met the cattle agent while the boys grazed the herd a few miles outside town. "The buyers generally drove out to look at the herds," recalled rancher John Clay. "In the afternoon we would meet, have a drink or two and find out what had been done through the day. We got supper about six o'clock. The cigars were lighted. Gradually the Texas crowd would concentrate, go across the tracks, all sit around in a circle and hold a council of war, smoking, chewing, whittling, comparing notes, forming embryo trusts. . . . The buyers did the same, only they were not so well organized as their southern neighbors. Then we met, had conflabs together and gradually trades were made and the cattle began to travel northward."

Often it took only a few hours to sell the herd. The boys penned it in the buyer's lot, then headed for town.

If there was time for a prank before the serious fun began, cowboys were adept at spoofing themselves as well as their visitors. While moving a herd through Nebraska in 1883, Teddy Blue Abbott thrilled a few Union Pacific passengers by stuffing a dummy with grass and hanging it over a telephone pole. As the train slowed at the depot, the boys showered the dummy with bullets. When one of them clipped the rope with a shot, Teddy grabbed up the loose end and rode off across the prairie with the "body" trailing behind. "The people on the train were scared to death," he chortled. "Women fainted and children screamed. They begged the conductor to pull

Roping cattle takes skill,
is work cowboys like best. Here Gary
Morton ropes "hard & fast"
with honda (slipknot) around saddle horn.
When he loops head, horns, or hind legs,
horse digs in, line tautens, calf
is thrown. Opposite: Morton switches
rope overhead to avoid tangle as
calf crosses behind him.

out before we held up the train." The stunt was such a success that even as the boys gloated over the easterners' gullibility, the sheriff, the coroner, and their boss arrived "just foaming."

Most of the fun-starved drovers finished off the day in a saloon. Texas Street in Abilene was a "glowing thoroughfare which led from the dreariness of the open prairies straight into the delight of Hell itself," observed one prim witness. It was the home of the saloons and dance halls, the residence of dozens of the "soiled doves of the Plains." Atmospheric places when the lights burned low and the music grew loud, the saloons faded in attractiveness and glamour under the unpleasant glare of the Dodge City photographers. Often no more than a tent or shanty in the early days, the saloons housed bad liquor and provided a welcome for the seedy cow hands who did not feel at home on the proper side of town.

By evening the saloons and gambling houses were running full tilt. With three months' pay in their pockets, the cowboys set out to forget the hardship and loneliness of the trail. Besides, they had to have something to brag to their friends about after they returned home. An evening's entertainment at the famous Long Branch Saloon in Dodge City might have consisted of a concert by "Professor" Miller and his four-piece orchestra. After 1878 they could have heard Dodge City's well-known cowboy band. Most saloons at least offered music—a piano player, a singer, or maybe just a music box. Sometimes a ballad singer or a comic might belt out a risqué song if business slowed down. Dodge City even imported four Mexican bullfighters for one Fourth of July program.

One show that played to various cowboy audiences across the Midwest was the Lord Dramatic Company, which first opened in Kansas in 1869. James A. and Louie Lord dazzled cowmen, she with her fake golden curls that hung down to her waist, until his death in 1885, when his son Edward took over the company. More popular was comic Eddie Foy, who first played Dodge City in 1878. Also a singer and dancer, Foy was a newcomer to the West who thought the thousands of buffalo bones he saw en route to Dodge were bones of citizens who died so fast the undertakers could not bury them. He proved his good character to the punchers when, after a series of facetious jokes that offended the cowboys, he good-naturedly endured their roughhousing.

The proper side of town was always separated from the red-light district by the railroad track. If the cowboy minded his manners he could venture across the tracks and catch an infrequent performance of **Macbeth** or perhaps **Uncle Tom's Cabin,** but he might have been as intellectually ill-prepared as the cowboy who, on seeing Lady Macbeth, stood up and complained that "she had her shimmy on." The editor of the Dodge City newspaper might have spoken for all the cowmen when he observed that "there are several kinds of culture, and from the different varieties we must select that which will be of practical use, together with a portion of that which is ornamental. Say we have two-thirds useful culture and one third ornamental," he continued. "We do not want all of one kind, especially if that kind is of the ornamental variety."

After an evening of drinking, gambling, and show-going, many cowboys chose to top it off with a visit to their favorite "nymph du prairie." Western prostitutes have long been famous, although little specific information about them is available because cowboys and others of their customers were silenced by Victorian morality if not by common sense. Charles M. Russell painted his "Sunshine Series" for the Silver Dollar Saloon in Great Falls, Montana, in 1898 to entertain the bar's rowdier customers. Russell portrayed the cowboy in a sympathetic and humorous light as he showed the hardships of the trail leading to the delicacies of the bawdy house, which resulted in a rather common ailment and a painful remedy.

For years Russell's little watercolors were among the most explicit information available on the girls who followed the trail herds from town to town, but Teddy Blue Abbott proved at least as knowledgeable on the subject when his memoirs appeared in 1939. Abbott was a short, steely-eyed Englishman raised in the West. His tanned good looks were probably a welcome relief from the craggy, bewhiskered scarfaces most of the girls usually saw. "In Miles City that summer [1884] I found a lot of new friends and some old ones," Abbott began. "There was girls there that I had seen at a lot of different places along the trail. The madams would bring them out from Omaha and Chicago and St. Paul; you would see them in Ogallala, and then again in Cheyenne or the Black Hills."

Teddy Blue was particularly adept at entertaining his colleagues with jokes, rhymes, and stories about the girls. He had met the well-known Calamity Jane in the Black Hills in 1878, and when he ran into her again in Miles City, he could not resist playing a trick on his employer, the owner of the F U F Ranch. "I'll give you two dollars and a half if you'll go and sit on his lap and kiss him," he offered Calamity. "And she was game. She walked up to him with everybody watching her, and sat down on his lap and throwed both her arms around him so his arms were pinned to his sides and he couldn't help himself—she was strong as a bear. And then she began kissing him and saying: 'Why don't you ever come to see me any more, honey? You know I love you.'" Teddy enjoyed his joke, telling the embarrassed rancher to go "ahead and have a good time. . . . I won't write home and tell your folks about it."

Teddy Blue won his nickname in perhaps his supreme stunt. As he headed to a back room with one of the girls at Turner's Theater in Miles City, he walked behind the stage, snagged his spur on the carpet, and fell through a small partition onto the stage. "Well, I thought, if you're before an audience you've go to do something, so I grabbed a chair from one of the musicians and straddled it and bucked it all around the stage, yelling, 'Whoa Blue! Whoa Blue!'—which was a cowpuncher expression at that time." The name stuck. "Teddy Blue I have been for fifty-five years," he concluded.

When not chinning with the girls, Teddy Blue was making up rhymes about them. "Cowboy Annie was her name,/And the N Bar outfit was her game," he wrote during a trip back to the cow camp. "And when the beef is four years old,/We'll fill her pillow slips with gold." He created quite a sensation by riding into camp with the stocking of his girl friend tied around

"A party of playful cowboys" terrorizing passengers of captured Southern Pacific train, near Uvalde, TX, 1886. Ruffianly side of cowboys occasionally persisted.

Following pages: MC herd crossing Oregon high desert en route to winter grazing. Cattle start and end day bunched up, but are encouraged to "string out" while moving. Bunched cattle get overheated, go too slowly. With smaller crews these days, six men may control 500 head.

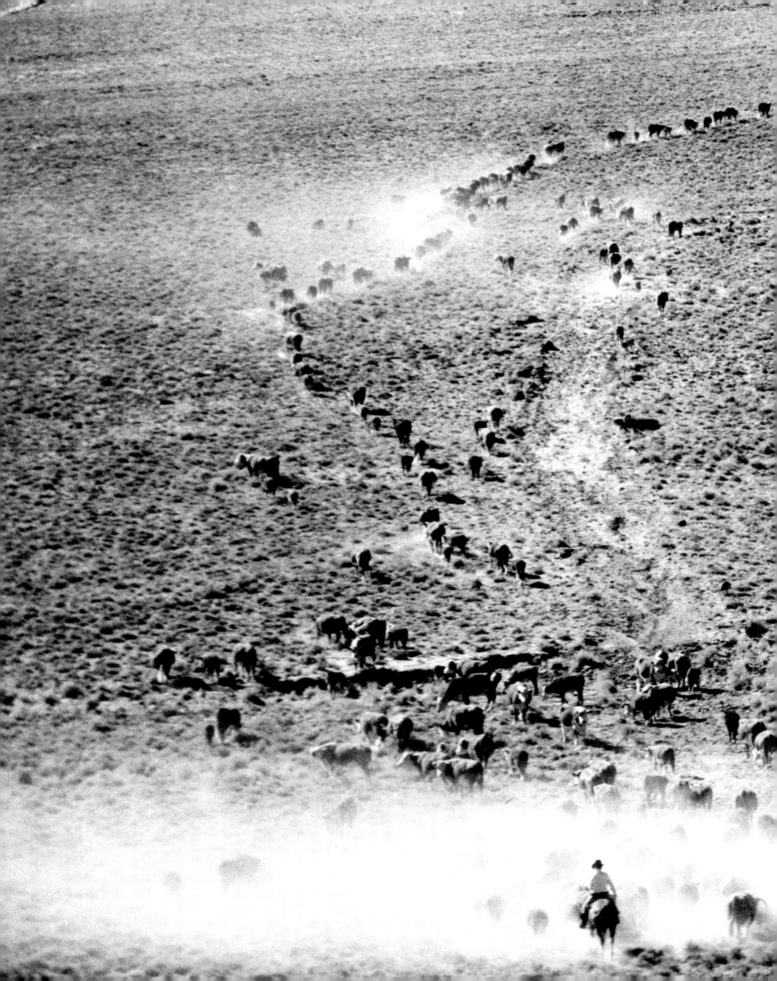

his arm "like the knights of old." But even Abbott, quick and handsome as he was, was no match for the experienced girls of the western brothels: "The girls said I was the best-looking cowboy on Powder River," he remembered, "and they cleaned me down to my spurs."

Although few cowboy reminiscences are as candid as Abbott's, most of the cowboys knew the girls even if they did not patronize them. The brass checks stamped "Compliments of Miss Olga" or some such and often bearing a fair likeness of the girl on the back were often considered legal tender on the trail, selling for about a dollar.

An evening's entertainment might have led to a confrontation with the town marshal. The girls often played a cowboy from one outfit off against a cowboy from another outfit, with the prize being the right to "marry" her for a week. Such stakes sometimes led to bitter fights, even among cowboys who normally avoided a brawl. "Cowboys are good-hearted and kind, sympathetic and not looking for trouble if it can be avoided," said McCauley, "but nevertheless, when nothing but trouble will do, you have struck the right party when you strike the average cowboy." Eastern reporters were not so generous in their opinion. "When 'off duty' cowboys are a terror in the way they manifest their exuberance of spirits," commented a correspondent for **Leslie's** in 1882. "Veteran settlers and stage-drivers regard them as the incarnation of devilry, and everybody fears them. They practice a kind of guerrilla warfare during their brief and infrequent holidays in the towns."

Several cattle towns finally took steps to curtail their activity. They hired well-known gunmen to face down the ruffians. James Butler ("Wild Bill") Hickok replaced Thomas J. ("Bear River Tom") Smith, whose short five-month tenure ended when a farmer chopped off his head with an ax. Wyatt Earp served as an officer (never marshal) in Wichita and Dodge City, and William B. ("Bat") Masterson spent a little time as sheriff in Dodge. City councils passed stringent laws, intended more to make money than to force acceptable behavior on the cowboys. Drovers entering Abilene in the summer of 1870 were confronted with a sheaf of new city ordinances: "To Prevent Gambling," "Respecting Vagrancy," "To Regulate the sale of Spirituous Intoxicating Liquors," "To Prohibit Drunkeness and Disorderly Conduct," "Relating to the Carrying of Fire Arms and other Deadly Weapons," "Relating to Houses of Ill-Fame," and if that were not enough, a final one "Relating to Sundry Offences." One historian found that more than half the income of Caldwell, Kansas, resulted from enforcement of such ordinances, usually against cowboys who populated the town during the summer months.

It is not hard to see that the usual drover returned to Texas broke, having spent his hard-earned cash on handsome clothes, and wine, women, and song, explaining why the boss usually included a return-trip railroad ticket as part of his pay.

The frequent post-Civil War trail drives from Texas to Kansas were a new development in the cattle trade, and a new type of cowboy resulted. The trail drives distinguished the cowboys from mere ranch hands. Ranch hands consumed time building fence, fixing fence, riding fence. They stayed close to the ranch year round, taking care of the innumerable chores.

112

Range boss entertains hands with story around chuck-wagon fire, near Tascosa, TX, 1908.

"This was a better job than I had been having," admitted McCauley, "but I wanted to go with the outfit where they didn't do anything but drive cattle." Abner Blocker definitely would have agreed with McCauley. "I got down on my knees," he said on an especially exuberant occasion, "and promised God Almighty that if I ever planted another cottonseed I would first boil it for three days so as to make sure it would never come up." McCauley and Blocker represented the new cowboy who grew to maturity on the trail, appreciating a different culture, with adventure in his soul, and wanderlust a dominant thought. And it was in Abilene, a result of the trail drives, that the "Texas cowboy was discovered and first became a distinct type, and here he first displayed for a national audience those extremes of temperament that make a hero," concluded a latter-day aficionado.

Most cowboys remembered the trail drive as the highlight of their career. For many it was the only cowboying all year, unsatisfactorily mingled with other jobs during the winter months. A man might spend only a few years in the saddle, but they were formative years. "I wouldn't take anything for what I have saw, but I wouldn't care to travel the same road again," concluded McCauley. Almost without exception, the old cowhands who wrote their memoirs devoted a generous section to this most glamorous event, as if it were the trail drive that certified a genuine cowboy. Although at seventy-eight he had resided in one of the best cattle sections of Montana, having married the daughter of one of the wealthiest cattlemen there, Teddy Blue Abbott saw his life force shaped by the three trail drives he made. "Those years were what made a cowboy of me," he recalled. "Nothing could have changed me after that."

Similarly, many who knew the cowboy first-hand insist that the real cowboy vanished with the trail drive. The specific skills still exist—even in improved form, if the Rodeo Cowboy Association record book is any example. But the trail drive and its folkways build no more men. "The brown heerds and wild men that [Francis] Parkman knew and told of so well have gon," Charles Russell wrote his friend W. M. Armstrong in 1921. "The long horned spotted cows that walked the same trails their humped backed cousins made have joined them in history, and with them went the wether worn cow men. They live now onley in bookes. The cow puncher of Forty years ago is as much history as Parkmans Tralper."

Most of the acts identified with cowboying took place in preparation for or during the drive. The campfire, memorialized in paintings and verse and feted in folklore, was the center of a robust community life. Even today a bright blaze seems to provoke conviviality among recalcitrant cowhands who have played the strong and silent part all day. There the humorous twist of mind and articulateness unique to their speech reveal

Opposite: Rest break
for man and horse during branding.
Stirrup is over saddle horn because
cinch has been loosened.
Note Bell brand on horse's shoulder.
Gear: Texas cowboy's shotgun chaps—
pronounced ''shaps''—and small
spurs (l), buckaroo horn wrapped
in rawhide; split reins (top) are joined
in romal—quirt, Montana
cowboy's buckaroo saddle
and chink chaps.

themselves. Perhaps it was the solitude, the "nearness of the stars, the bigness of the country, and the far horizons" which enabled him "to think clearly and go into the depths of his own mind," speculated Ramon Adams, who has studied the cowboy for decades. Regardless, the cowboy is not "hog-tied when it comes to makin' chin music" around the campfire, and his tongue might become "plumb frolicsome." "The campfire is to all outdoor life what the evening fireside is to domestic life," Andy Adams philosophized. "After the labors of the day are over, the men gather around the fire, and the social hour of the day is spent in yarning. The stories told may run from the sublime to the ridiculous, from a true incident to a base fabrication, or from a touching bit of pathos to the most vulgar vulgarity."

The campfire reveals surprising wit in the most unlikely punchers and is the seminar in which the contemporary oral tradition of the range is passed on. One Montana cowboy who supposedly couldn't "have two many things on his mind at once" proved himself to be a poetic declaimer around the campfire, rendering "The Face On the Barroom Floor" and several other "cowboy classics" in a staccato delivery that left his friends gasping at his memory.

Closely related is the cowboy's humor, whether as illustrated in Russell's painting of the **Bronc in Cow Camp,** with a puncher riding the bucking horse through the fire watchers, or in the countless presentations of "son-of-a-bitch stew," a range delicacy that apparently could be eaten only in ignorance of its contents. The cowboys had no radios or "canned" entertainment, explained Abbott, so they created their own. "That was why I got such a reputation among them for singing and storytelling and all that foolishness," he recalled. "It might be a rainy night and they would all be humped up around the camp fire, feeling gloomy, and I'd come in and tell some cock and bull story about my bad breaks at theaters or what I'd done or what I was going to do, and in a minute I'd have them all laughing. Veto Cross, who was our boss coming up from the North Platte in '83, used to say I was worth forty dollars a month just to stick around camp."

Some cowboys fought the loneliness of the trail with more serious pursuits. Often they could not read their month-old copy of the **Police Gazette** because they worked until the sun went down, but they could use the light of the campfire to write in the ever-present diary (judging from the number ultimately published), or to write home or to a sweetheart. Others played poker, using yearlings at fifty cents a head and top steers at $5 per head as chips. "I carried brush and corn-stalks and anything I could get to make a light for those who were on guard to play poker by," recalled young Lee Moore. "My compensation for light was twenty-five cents per night or as long as the game lasted. Every few days they would divide up and brand and each man take his cattle home."

The campfire, then, was the cowboy's place, his home away from home. It was the seat of hospitality, the seat of entertainment for visitors. "It's your property," explained Teddy Blue, "and if a stranger rides up you say: 'Come into camp and sit down,' just the way you do in a house." The campfire also is the center of an outfit's jurisdiction, which spreads in a radius

Few leisure hours in
cowboys' seven-day week
on range are spent
playing poker, throwing
rope in elimination
game called "Horse," and
bathing with hats on.

of a hundred feet. "If you order a man out of camp you can't order him no further than that," said Teddy.

Grade B western movies did little more for the cowboy than promote his image as a singer on the trail. Gene Autry might have sung for the heroine, but the real cowboy sang for his own amusement, and to lull the cattle. He picked up songs from different parts of the country or wrote his own as he coddled the cattle through the night. "I learned 'The Little Black Bull' first," recalled Teddy. "That's the oldest song on the range. They say it came out of the Ozark mountains and you'll notice it talks about oxen in the second verse. It don't mention steers." Songs that are seriously regarded as folk art today were the objects of fun for the cowboy. "I always had to stop and laugh every time I sang the Laredo song, in spite of it being so sad," continued Teddy. "Because first he is lying there dead, wrapped up in his blanket, and then he starts in telling this big long story of his life and how he met his downfall."

Regardless of which drover diary one reads, the trip north is described in terms of rivers forded, prairie monotony, dangers overcome, heroic effort expended—but it was more. It was an Experience, beginning in South Texas and climaxing in the cattle towns of Abilene, Dodge City, Cheyenne. At their height the trail drives might be compared to today's rush-hour traffic jams, because the trails were full, the resources stretched to the point of exhaustion. Teddy Blue Abbott must have thought he lived at the most auspicious moment in history that day in 1883 when he was out hunting some horses. "I rode up on a little hill to look for the horses, and from the top of the hill I could see seven herds behind us; I knew there were eight herds ahead of us, and I could see the dust from thirteen more of them on the other side of the river." Richard King, patriarch of the giant King Ranch of South Texas, had as many as six herds on the trail at one time.

Much of the cowboy character, maybe even the American character, developed on those expeditions known as trail drives that crossed the Plains with such regularity. Respect for authority combined with western egalitarianism to confuse certain military-minded writers who studied the trail camp. The trail boss was absolute boss, but could relinquish much of his authority without compromising his respect among the men. The democracy of the campfire spawned some of America's best colloquialisms. "There ain't much paw and beller to a cowboy," went one such puncher saying. "The bigger the mouth the better it looks shut."

That cowboying is hard work is evident: the early morning rising, the monotony of the drive, the stampedes, the rivers, the deserts, the loneliness. But cowboys apparently like hard work, as their achievements and routine testify. "Nobody ever drowned himself in sweat," explained one who had ridden up the trail several times. Hamp Baker, a Palo Pinto County, Texas, trail hand, concluded that rounding up cattle was "a hot teadious task, and very wearisome." And while many denizens of the West still speak out articulately for the "old ways," they probably would all agree with Major George W. Littlefield of Austin, who after twenty years admitted he was "tired of the trail." "I shall be happy," he said, "to take the **rail** in the future."

121

the cattle barons

Million-acre western spreads would never have existed without risk-taking ranchers who put them together and watched over them with rigorous determination. They welded the wild cowboys, the wilder longhorns, and the immense public lands into a new industry that flavored the Gilded Age with a particularly frontier tinge. Richard King capitalized spectacularly on a few hundred dollars' worth of Santa Gertrudis Country. Charles Goodnight surveyed all the eye could see in Palo Duro Canyon and swore at that moment to have it for his dream ranch. The State of Texas granted the famous XIT Ranch more than 3,000,000 acres of public domain for one of the largest cattle empires ever to exist. "The immensity of the continent produces a kind of intoxication," observed a nineteenth-century Englishman. "There is moral dram-drinking in the contemplation of the map. No Fourth of July orator can come up to the plain facts contained in the Land Commissioner's report."

Legend insists it all began by accident. Supposedly an emigrant headed west with several yoke of oxen was caught in an eastern Wyoming snowstorm and forced to abandon them with his wagons. Certain that they had perished, he returned the following spring with another team to salvage his cargo. To his surprise, he found the oxen living, fat and healthy, near the wagons. They had survived the winter by feeding on the wild grasses frozen beneath the snow. Only then, according to the myth, did the cowmen realize that Plains grass was good the year around, rather than just when green or when dried as hay, as were the eastern grasses. Countless nineteenth-century moguls knew that "there's gold from the grass roots down," related a guide from Dakota's gold country in the 1870s, but only a few shrewd cattlemen foresaw the "gold from the grass roots up."

Regardless of how it began, the two decades following the Civil War witnessed the birth of a new industry, a new American legend, and the ultimate change of a country's eating habits. Gutsy cowboys developed into a class of men unprecedented in determination, ability, and grit. Understanding that the right combination of material would produce a profitable business, these entrepreneurs extracted wealth from the Great American Desert. Two kinds of men—and all combinations in between—directed this new livestock industry: the cowboy and the businessman. Twenty-six-year-old John W. Iliff was one of the first businessmen. Together with Charles Goodnight, one of the first cowboy-ranchers, he built an empire in Colorado. An alumnus of Ohio Wesleyan College, Iliff headed west with a $500 stake given him by his father. He struggled in "bleeding" Kansas for a year before moving to Colorado, where gold had been discovered in 1858. There he opened a store in Cherry Creek. Because so many would-be miners had nothing to do with their oxen after reaching the gold fields, Iliff began a "cattle ranch" and purchased the oxen. When Colorado Territory was created in 1861, he foresaw the development of Denver and expanded his business. At first he simply grazed the exhausted cattle on the rich Colorado grass for a year to sell them. Then he bought bulls to breed his own herd.

Indians usually hampered ranchers, but they helped Iliff.

Opening pages: Starting
out to make afternoon
circle during fall roundup
on 06's, Alpine, TX.

A neighboring fur trader who had married an Indian chief's twin daughters warned him when a raid was likely. As Indian depredations increased in Wyoming, the mail route shifted southward, bringing Iliff more business. And when the troopers rode westward to drive the Indians onto reservations, Iliff sold beef to the government contractors. By the time the railroad came, increasing the beef market even more, he was a wealthy man who controlled a large part of the Colorado cattle industry. Thus he was in a position to contract for $40,000 worth of cattle from the young Charles Goodnight in 1867, when Goodnight pushed his first herd up the newly blazed Goodnight-Loving Trail.

Goodnight was typical of the cowboys who became ranchers. As he drove steers up the trail to Colorado and Wyoming, he purchased bits of land along the Arkansas River near Pueblo. He made enough money to move to Colorado and begin his own ranch. By 1870 he had given up trailing cattle. He soon found that ranching in the northern lands was different from Texas and changed his methods. In Texas the cattle cared for themselves until the long drive to market. In Colorado the rancher purchased Texas cattle and fattened them for sale, providing forage in the winter and making sure that they were protected from the cold. Instead of hiring temporary, roughneck hands for the trail, Goodnight employed men who knew cattle and could be counted on to see them through the difficulties of a normal Colorado winter.

Nor was selling the cattle as easy as it had been in Texas. Texas cattle were worth virtually the same no matter when they were sold. Cattle fattened in Colorado fluctuated greatly in price, depending on demand, and if the rancher chose the wrong time to sell he could lose thousands of dollars. The ranch manager of South Dakota's VVV Ranch estimated that he lost some $10,000 by waiting two weeks to sell one herd.

Goodnight also learned to ranch on credit, something that soon became as necessary as the thousands of acres of open land. In the early days credit was extended for the asking. Drovers from Texas took other ranchers' cattle to market, then remembered how much to pay them when they returned. No notes or contracts were signed. Contracts became necessary as the industry became more complex, and cattlemen began to give promissory notes, which were sold to banks at discounts. This led banks to make loans directly on cattle. Soon credit was a necessity for a man to start a ranch.

Dislike of the two percent interest rate on borrowed money doomed Goodnight's first fortune. To avoid paying the interest, he went into the banking business himself, organizing the Stock Grower's Bank of Pueblo. He might have succeeded but for the fact that he began banking the same month that the depression of 1873 hit the country. It "wiped me off the face of the earth," he later told a friend. He then overstocked his ranch in an effort to retrieve his losses, and ultimately lost most of his money and cattle.

Goodnight gradually gathered reserve energy to begin a new ranch. He had not yet made his most important contributions to ranching, but his greatest diplomacy and managerial skill were required to reenter the business. He returned to Texas with his few cattle to establish his ranch in beautiful Palo Duro Canyon. The following year he invited young John and

Cornelia Adair, investment brokers whom he had met in Denver, out for a visit. After several weeks of the bracing air and West Texas scenery, laced with buffalo hunts and Goodnight's vision of a new ranch, Adair was ready to invest his money. For nearly one-half million of Adair's dollars, Goodnight gave him a share of the ranch and named it the JA.

Again proving that he was a good rancher, Goodnight purchased enough land to control the entire Palo Duro Canyon, built more than fifty houses across the ranch, including a two-story brick home for when the Adairs visited, purchased $150,000 worth of bulls, and gradually built up a herd of 100,000 cattle. Using organizational skills developed on the range and back in Colorado, Goodnight founded the first cattlemen's association in the Texas Panhandle. He designed a stirrup that protected the rider's foot when the horse fell, a new chuck box for the chuck wagon, and a sidesaddle. He even bred cattle and buffalo, producing what he called "cattalo," which he believed made superior meat and a more durable animal, but which so often died at birth that the experiment had to be discontinued. With astute management he earned more than $500,000 profit for Adair in five years.

Goodnight's success and Adair's profit clearly encouraged other foreigners to invest in western ranches. Another factor was the unusual western landscape. What could seem vaster or more gorgeous to a space-deprived Scot or New Englander than central and eastern Montana and Wyoming? For years they had read rhapsodic accounts of the West, such as this one penned by James Bell in 1854: "The low mountains which surround us are just far enough away to keep the eye from waring [wearying] with the desert wast while the rich coloring of the sky, combined with the whole landscape make any one who had 'music in the soul' wish to be a Painter, and any Painter wish for the power to coppy it." A group of West Texas cattlemen added steamboats plying the Pecos River to Bell's picture to complete the idealistic view of the desert. The governor of Wyoming pointed out that the West was more than beautiful. Its dry atmosphere would not conduct electricity or heat, he claimed, "so that exposed animals better retain their animal heat and keep their vital forces in full reserve."

In addition to the striking deserts, the West contained real beauty spots. Charles Russell could hardly believe his eyes when he first visited the South Fork of the Judith River in 1882. "Shut off from the outside world, it was a hunter's paradise, bounded by walls of mountains and containing miles of grassy open spaces, more green and beautiful than any man-made parks," he later wrote. "These parks and the mountains behind them swarmed with deer, elk, mountain sheep, and bear, besides beaver and other small fur-bearing animals. The creeks were alive with trout. Nature had surely done her best, and no king of the old times could have claimed a more beautiful and bountiful domain." Such land was natural cow country, and Russell soon had his first job as a night wrangler. "I was considered pretty worthless," he recalled, "but in spite of that fact I held their bunch, which consisted of 200 saddle horses. This life suited me."

Russell had begun his image-setting career. His work as a night wrangler left him free to sketch and draw during most of the day. By

1885 he had attracted some local attention with his watercolors and oils, being certain to show Montana as "God's country" even in the pictures which depicted his friends riding bucking broncos or working a herd.

Another westerner gained a different kind of publicity for the ranch land. General James S. Brisbin summarized his view of ranching in a promotional piece entitled, **The Beef Bonanza, or How to Get Rich on the Plains,** in 1881. Profit was easy in ranching, he noted, but perhaps the most attractive feature was the small amount of capital required to get into business. Two hundred dollars would purchase a headquarters site almost anywhere in the West. Two hundred more would buy the necessary tools. A small cash reserve would take care of any wages and salaries that had to be paid to the cowboys, while the bulk of the investment could be put directly into livestock. General Brisbin estimated that $25,000 would set the new rancher up with 1,750 cows and enough good bulls to breed. After six years the novice could expect a net profit of more than $50,000 plus compound interest on the original investment of $25,000.

Little wonder that easterners and foreigners were so anxious to spend their money in the West. Britishers had been investing in the United States since 1815, with the California gold rush heightening the interest in the West. John Adair had shown by investing in Goodnight's Texas Panhandle ranch that there was money to be made, but little more than promises were needed to start the flow of money with such ecstatic accounts to read as had already been published about the West. Nor did the money all come from wealthy individuals, for the British Parliament had made it possible—with the legalization of investment trusts—for small investors to buy into western ranching. The Scottish-American Mortgage Company, Limited, of Edinburgh secured land mortgages in Illinois, and a Dundee group loaned money on northwestern land, and received twelve and a half to fifteen percent interest, because they could legally charge higher rates in America than Britain. Their success, plus the built-in romanticism of the West and ranching, guaranteed huge investments in the coming years. More than thirty British companies certified their intentions of investing money in American ranching between 1879 and 1888.

Eastern Americans also invested in the western venture. Theodore Roosevelt put $82,500 in his Dakota Badlands ranch, stock, and equipment in less than a year during the mid-1880s, just as ranching was entering its worst financial period. Others were just as eager to partake of what was rapidly becoming the most "American" of industries. A Kentucky corporation operated the Two Buckle Ranch in Texas, and a Chicago firm put money into the Dubuque Cattle Company in New Mexico.

Probably the best-known foreign-controlled ranch was the famous XIT in West Texas. Reportedly named when a cowboy stooped and scratched "XIT" in the dirt with a stick and suggested that it stand for the ten counties that made up the ranch, the XIT was established by a Chicago firm that received state land in return for building the state capitol building in Austin. Founded in 1885, the ranch was soon home to more than 110,000 cattle that quickly bred to more than 150,000. A few years later the syndicate

Driving 6666's cattle under the Big Sky.

Cross-country trail drive to railhead survives, but is limited by fencing. These days cattle buyers usually go to ranch, truck their purchases away. On 06's, cattle are shifted to pens by Ranch Manager Chris Lacy and hand (top), then guided up ramp into truck while manager, owner, buyer, and old 06 cowboy talk deal. Buyer figures price on hand calculator.

Huge, famous, little-seen King Ranch, 1939-44. Left: Photographer Toni Frissell climbed windmill to get perfect picture of point, swing (flank), and drag riders moving a herd. Center: Branding takes place in midsummer heat. Right: King Ranch quarter horse mares and foals entering corral.

established a "finishing" ranch in Montana where the Texas beeves could be wintered while they fattened.

But western ranching contained unseen pitfalls. A Pennsylvania-born cattleman named Alexander Hamilton Swan promoted the deal that seduced a group of thrifty Scotsmen in Edinburgh to invest their money in his Swan Land and Cattle Company. Although Swan probably did not conceive the deal as a swindle, he surely made an error in the number of cattle on his land. The "book count" far exceeded the actual number of cattle on the range, a usual situation because it was virtually impossible to count all the cattle scattered over an area as large as Scotland itself. The Scottish company paid Swan more than $2,300,000 for his holdings. The following year the company paid another $2,300,000 for railroad land that enabled them to control much more of the range than they actually owned—typical cattle-baron procedure.

For a few years the venture seemed ideal, even to untrusting Scotsmen watching their investment. They controlled more than 3,250,000 acres of land and owned so many brands that their foreman had to have his own brand book to recognize the company stock. They paid everyday cowhands as much as $45 per month, an almost unheard-of figure in 1884. The investors, meanwhile, were reaping dividends of as much as twenty-five percent in 1883, 1884, and 1885.

Such profits obviously attracted others. Even ranches that had no history of profit were sold to dashing foreigners who succumbed to the lure of the wide-open spaces or the belief that their managerial skill could turn a losing situation around. The Maxwell Cattle Company, Limited, eventually encompassed almost 2,000,000 acres of northeast New Mexico and southeastern Colorado, and Britishers who owned the Espuela (Spur) Land and Cattle Company, near the High Plains of Texas, counted almost a million acres of dry West Texas turf as theirs. Development of the Espuela Ranch is typical of the big ranches. The Spur was a corporation made up of several westerners, headed by A. M. Britton of Denver, who had also developed the famous Matador Ranch of West Texas and sold out at a handsome profit to a Scotch syndicate. The group bought thousands of acres of ranch land, then Britton headed to England to find investors who would "buy at once and repent at leisure," as had apparently become the custom in Britain. He soon found gentlemen willing to organize the Espuela Land and Cattle Company, Limited, of London, and sold them the Spur Ranch in 1885. A "book count" of 40,000 cattle was included in the deal. Unlike the Swan Company, which soon experienced difficulty in finding all the stock it was supposed to have, both the Maxwell Land Company and the Espuela Land and Cattle Company were profitably run by efficient managers who kept good

records and were not afraid of a visit from the stockholders.

Sons and relatives of American industrial titans turned to ranching as an outlet for their money and energy: William Rockefeller, brother of John D.; Alexander Agassiz, son of the naturalist Louis; William K. Vanderbilt; Russell B. Harrison, son of the President, and many others. But probably the most colorful career on the range belonged to Antoine-Amédee-Marie-Vincent Mance de Vallambrosa, better known as the Marquis de Mores. He left his native France and established a fabulous ranch in the Bad Lands of North Dakota, where he was neighbor to Theodore Roosevelt. Stopping in New York City long enough to take Mendora von Hoffman, daughter of a rich banker, as his bride, the Marquis established the town of Mendora on the Little Missouri River, and built a twenty-six-room château staffed with twenty servants. He idled his time away in his English-German-French library or on hunting trips. He traveled in his private Pullman, or, as he described it, his "live-in hunting coach." For a brief moment, the West might have been the paradise the foreigners expected, for the Marquis dabbled in gardening, dairying, gold mining, and even started a stage line between Mendora and Deadwood. They built "castles on the prairies," reported the English paper **The Economist.**

One psychological characteristic shared by almost all the cattle barons was a sense of community. They talked to and about each other, relishing the extravagances—of economy or wealth—of their breed. Moreton Frewen was not just a failure, but a "sublime failure." As part owner of the Powder River Cattle Company, he often astonished his neighbors by sending cut flowers to his ranch or riding miles across the Plains in a snowstorm to be on time for a dinner party. The neighbors probably appreciated the rumor that he once bought the same herd of cattle twice more than the other stories about him. He reportedly bought the herd the first time when shown the cattle, and a second time after the seller drove them behind a hill and presented them again. Some cattlemen loved to spend money, but others, trained in economy, could not change their ways after they became wealthy. "He'd skin a flea for its hide and tallow," said one rancher raconteur, "but he ain't as near as he used to be." A wealthy San Angelo, Texas, cattleman claimed that he did not need to change from his tattered work clothes while in Texas because "everybody here knows me. . . . What difference does it make whether I'm dressed up or not?" Then, caught in Kansas City in the same ragged attire, he reacted: "Oh, pshaw, nobody up here knows me."

Cattlemen prided themselves on their accomplishments and intended, in several notable instances, to see that the world did not forget. Frenchman Pierre Wibaux built his most enduring monument in western banking, but memorialized himself with a bronze statue in the entrance of his

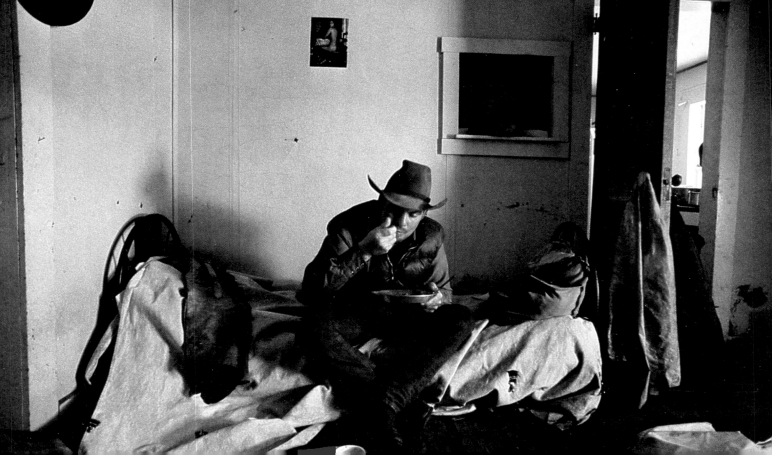

Top: Ranch Manager
J. J. Gibson and wife Nada
in main ranch house
of 6666's. Bottom: Wagon
Boss Kelly Fortune
at line camp of John Scott
Cattle Co., Billings, MT.

bank. Shanghai Pierce, who perhaps owned more cattle and less land (50,000 cattle on eleven acres) than any other cattleman, was reportedly as "uncouth as the cattle he drove," but had a grander vision of himself. As he neared death he commissioned a sculptor to do a statue—"a fair likeness of myself"—to be put over his grave so people would say there "stands" old Pierce. No doubt the image was in keeping with his response to one who asked if he belonged to the small church he established on his ranch. "Hell, no," retorted Pierce. "The church belongs to me."

Most of the cattle barons acted in a manner that eventually defined the term, for cattle barons created a new role in American society and took their seat beside the moguls of industry and latter-day Texas oilmen as leading espousers of individualism, free enterprise, and opportunity—or "opportunity for all, success to the best," as one rancher put it. Joseph McCoy summarized it after watching the best of the cattlemen trail their stock to Abilene: "Men who in their youth receive a thorough drilling in adversity, and thus not only learn the intrinsic value of a dollar but how to make and take care of one, invariably make earth's most successful business men."

Cattlemen themselves emphasized their "rags to riches" origins. McCoy cited Goodnight as one who came from poverty to wealth via cattle trading, but there were more dramatic examples. Denis Sheedy raised rabbits as a boy, then read Blackstone to improve himself. Although the cowboys thought of him as stingy, other cattlemen recognized him as a man who "finds the cheapest market when he buys, and the highest market when he sells." Californian Jerome Churchill claimed an even greater metamorphosis. "I never inherited anything from my parents, I helped support them before I was of age, and I supported them for years before they died," he claimed. Shanghai Pierce probably took great pride in the fact that he, a penniless lad when he came to Texas after the Civil War, was able to buy half interest in an Arkansas hotel on the spot when the clerk told him there were no rooms for rent.

Relishing their reputation for logical decisions and incisive enforcement, cattlemen played down their hard-nosed treatment of those outside their select circle. The story of the rancher who cheated a stranger in a horse trade, then justified his action by recourse to the Bible verse admonishing Christians to "take in" strangers is cheerily repeated. So are the countless tales which demonstrate the cattlemen's fundamental honesty by returning their neighbor's strayed stock. Perhaps the complex rancher mentality is best illustrated in the advertisement that appeared in the Tascosa (Texas) **Pioneer** in September, 1886: "Any person caught monkeying with any of my cattle without permission will catch Hell! Yours in Christ, Grizzley Calleen."

The cattlemen seemed willing and able to defend their "self-made" label. To them this meant that success, if not ranching, was in their blood. Teddy Roosevelt probably believed this; undoubtedly the European noblemen who invested in ranching accepted it as a fact of life. Cattlemen who did not believe that they were destined to be better than their fellow man might at least have believed that ranching was in their blood. Although many ranchers professed to be Christians, their code of self-reliance and

135

Some contemporary cowboys still carry firearms. Those who do generally want security while working alone in isolated locations. Rustlers now are motorized, are dealt with by cattlemen's association and range detectives.

individuality made it difficult for them to accept the traditional doctrine of salvation by grace. Owen Wister's Virginian, for example, claimed that he could "do nothing long enough and bad enough to be damned" if he could "do nothing long enough and good enough to earn eternal happiness."

During the formative years of the industry, cattlemen had either been able to ignore the law or write it. This led to conflict that both showed the cowmen's power and hurried the end of the era. When Charles Goodnight rode across the High Plains of Texas in 1876 and sighted Palo Duro Canyon for the first time, he realized that it was a cattleman's dream and determined to possess it for his ranch. He went about its acquisition in the manner approved by the code of the range. Using John Adair's money, he purchased or homesteaded only the most important tracts of land that controlled the water and provided a good site for headquarters. Since there was no water on the remaining land, no one occupied it, and it was left for Goodnight to use at his leisure. The ranchers had no way of acquiring other land, in fact, except through the hands of a second party. By the time cattlemen needed large tracts of land, the only way they could secure public domain was by homesteading (limit 160 acres), or by purchasing it from someone who had homesteaded it, or from the railroad, which had been awarded a section of western land for every mile of track built. Sometimes the ranchers had their cowhands homestead land, then turn it over to them for a small fee once all the legal requirements had been fulfilled.

More often the ranchers like Goodnight occupied the land and claimed it. Advertisements such as "I, the undersigned, do hereby notify the public that I claim the valley branching off the Glendive Creek four miles east of the Allard and extending to its source on the south side of the Northern Pacific Railroad as a stock range" were becoming common in western papers. Although such notices had no legal standing, they were part of the rancher's code and were enforced by the stockmen's associations. The land was held by possessory rights, cow custom, range privilege, accustomed range, range rights, or whatever the local cowmen agreed to call it. This meant that land sold by a rancher had been occupied by that rancher, and that the same right by which he held the land was transmitted to the new owner. The Coad brothers of Nebraska made no pretense that they owned all the land they sold for $912,853. The deed clearly stated that they owned only 527 acres that gave them control of the water. The other almost 150,000 acres the Coads held only by "possessory title or right thereto."

Other cattlemen gained control of double the amount of land they purchased by buying from the railroad. The public domain given the railroads by the Federal government formed a checkerboard pattern across the West, because the sections alternated on either side of the track. The ranchers would buy several sections, then fence their land, thereby enclosing the public domain lying between their sections.

One rancher who believed in purchasing all the land he used was Richard King, who bought his first parcel of pasture along the Santa Gertrudis Creek in 1853. Supposedly on the advice of Colonel Robert E. Lee, who might have visited the ranch while he was in Texas prior to the Civil War,

King bought land but never sold it. Because his empire-to-be was located in the relatively unsettled portion of South Texas, his original purchases were rather cheap. A few years after he started ranching, for example, he paid $600 for a purebred stallion, more money than he had paid for his original ranch. By the time of his death in 1885, King had amassed more than 500,000 acres of the prime grassland that formed the nucleus for the 1,500,000-acre spread of today.

Because the ranch lands were concentrated mainly in the western states and territories, cattlemen became accustomed to being ignored by Congress, a situation that led to conflict since the ranchers used the public domain, which Congress administered. The ranchers quickly formed cattlemen's associations, which were in reality extra-legal groups that administered the agreed-upon code among the membership. Ever since President Thomas Jefferson had so eulogized the agrarian/yeoman tradition, the laws of the United States favored the small landholder, particularly when disposing of the huge amounts of public domain. The cattlemen's associations facilitated the conduct of business on the range and protected the individual members and their property.

Conspicuously absent from this protection were the thousands of settlers who began the westward trek after the Civil War. Cattlemen who required vast amounts of land for their stock and who had invested so much money and work in the range naturally hated to see settlers moving onto the land and taking advantage of the laws to occupy it. The ranchers also considered the farmer a basically inferior being. "Some of our 'Nestors' [nesters] are making preparations for farming by building temporary brush fences," wrote the editor of the Fort Griffin **Echo.** "I think they are just wasting their time by trying to farm where cattle range by thousands and hogs by hundreds and nothing but brush to fence with which is liable to burn up at any time. Most of them are poor, having nothing to work with or to subsist on and in my judgment would be better off had they remained in the settlements where they could rent improved places." The manager of the Spur Ranch was even harsher in his opinion, claiming that they mavericked his stock. "The children ride bareback as soon as they can walk almost, and are continually itching to throw a rope on something when they are ten years old. From this class will be drawn the future inhabitants of the penitentiaries, and only a small percentage will be caught up with."

Even Goodnight's giant JA Ranch was troubled by settlers. His manager wrote that, "I am afraid we are going to be bothered a good deal by settlers coming in this year. Of course we have got nearly all the good land bought but these people are taking up rough land in the [Palo Duro] Canyon where we thought there was never any danger." His solution was just as forthright as his statement of the problem. "They just want it for shelter for their stock but they will be just like the others. We can buy them out in a few years."

The settlers, of course, presented just as logical an argument. They claimed the land legally according to the Homestead Act of 1862. The ranchers had used it freely for years, and should not be upset at finally having to give up such a small portion of their vast ranges. Some settlers, in fact, made it easier for the ranchers to expand their holdings, because they sold out after homesteading public domain, one of the only ways cattlemen could buy additional public land.

To protect the land from encroachers, the cattlemen soon fielded a new ally: barbed wire. They enclosed the public domain along with their land. One company in Colorado fenced in more than a million acres, including an entire village, which prompted the mail carrier to complain that "I must drive through such gates as they choose to put up." "Some morning we will wake up to find that a corporation has run a wire fence about the boundary lines of Wyoming," predicted the editor of the **Wyoming Sentinel,** "and all within the same have been notified to move." The ranchers made their wire hold with signs such as: "The man who opens the fence had better look out for his scalp," or anyone who cuts this fence "must be bulletproof."

Cattlemen who could not purchase the land had to resort to other means of controlling it. Some forced their cowboys to file for homesteads, then turn over the title when the requirements had been met. The ranchers would construct small "line shacks" on the homesteaded land to show evidence of settlement, and these shacks served as shelters for the cowboys as they rode their lonely route checking up on the cattle. Other cowmen encouraged soldiers' widows in the East to file for homesteads entitled to them under special land-bonus legislation, then bought the land from them for small sums of $200 to $400. Still others simply used fictitious names to file as many homesteads as they dared. One cowboy reportedly amassed more than 7,000 acres of land without being caught.

In the final analysis, the cattleman held his claim by violence and force. Settlers quickly realized that the ranchers had no ultimate claim to the land and protested. The cattlemen responded with the only weapons they had—force and the six-gun. Ugly incidents occurred in every ranching state as stock growers' associations sought to institutionalize the range law the cattlemen needed. Settlers who got too close to a stream were burned out. Stubborn farmers who refused to move might find a shriveled human ear tacked to their door or a hangman's noose on their doorsteps. When his peace-loving wife complained that some vigilantes had hanged some settlers from a telegraph pole, Charles Goodnight, who had known in advance of the plans for the hanging, replied, "Well, I don't think it hurt the telegraph pole."

The most spectacular confrontation between ranchers

Cattle (and sheep) men
have always warred
on coyote. One loser hangs
from fence in Davis
mountains of Big Bend.

and nesters was the so-called Johnson County range war in Wyoming in 1892. It makes little difference today who was on the right side, for it is a difficult matter to establish truth in the conflict now. Apparently goaded by the settlers, whom they thought to be rustling their stock, the cattlemen's association imported some fifty gunslingers from Texas to drive the settlers off the grazing land. The Texans rode to Wyoming in a tightly curtained railroad car then cut the telegraph lines to the town of Buffalo as they set out to chastise the settlers. Stopping en route to kill two "rustlers," they allowed the nesters time to organize and confront them just a few miles outside town. Heavily outnumbered, the Texans retreated to a nearby ranch and the cowmen cabled President Benjamin Harrison to send in Federal troops to prevent a lynching.

Although it seems that the ranchmen suffered a defeat, the farmers had not won a clear victory. After a brief hiatus in which the ranchers suffered the political consequences of their strong-arm tactics, the cattlemen's candidates were returned to office and in an amazing show of power they succeeded in preventing any publicity about the "war." One of the rarest of all Western books is Asa Shinn Mercer's **The Banditti of the Plains or the Cattlemen's Invasion of Wyoming in 1892: The Crowning Infamy of the Ages,** which the cattlemen succeeded in suppressing with a court injunction, then rounded up for a book-burning. A few copies survived the inferno, but the plates for the book were destroyed, and it was not reprinted until 1923 under a new title, **Powder River Invasion.** So complete was their purge that the cattlemen even got the copyright copies out of the Library of Congress. The story of the Johnson County war was not even popularized until Jack Schaefer's novel **Shane** (with the ensuing movie) in 1949.

The conflict was fierce because the cattlemen were fighting for a way of life that they had nurtured from nothing in 1867 to big business in 1885. The Wyoming Stock Grower's Association was perhaps the most powerful of the associations, beginning in 1873 with only ten members, but enlarging with the state's livestock industry. Unusual because it was organized even before the state's government, the association contained the most influential politicians and wealthiest individuals in the state, thereby wielding power far out of proportion to its numbers. Such associations performed useful functions in cow country, where organization was often the only way to stop or even slow a rustler or a "fast branding iron." But with the arrival of farmers and settlers, the cowmen's associations reacted toward them as they did toward any other encroacher, and the homesteader's perfectly legal occupation of the land was seen as a violation of the western code.

Ranching is often spoken of as a frontier institution. With the arrival of civilization, the very institution that made settlement possible ironically could no longer exist, except in radically changed form. Tactics that won the range proved heavy-handed or even illegal in a law-abiding population, and the rancher and his self-perpetuating code, admirable and idealistic from a distance, quickly proved themselves intolerable neighbors. While the major task performed by the rancher was the opening of the Great Plains, he is best known for his individualistic code that persists today as a part of the American image.

6

One fact that often eludes those interested in the drama and excitement of being a cowboy is that punching cattle is a tough, year-round job. It wasn't always so when the cowboy only worked during the spring and fall roundups and lazed around the ranch or a nearby town during the slack months. The cowboy's work originally consisted of rounding up the cattle, branding them, and getting them to market. During the peak season perhaps thirty hands might be required on a given ranch, whereas only ten or a dozen might be kept on during the summer and winter, when the work consisted of fence repair, breaking horses, and branding a few strays. This obviously uneconomic situation perplexed the efficiency-minded cattle barons until they established a rigid work pattern that lasted all year long. Ranches became more professional, and more businesslike managers and foremen took charge. Still, the cowboy was doing the only work in the world suitable to his independent nature, and those who believe that the chores actually tested his endurance find little evidence that he preferred any other kind of work.

To the cowboy work came in cycles, much like the school year might appear to a long-suffering professor who had no vacation. The high point of the year, of course, was arrival in the cow town in late summer, which was, in fact, graduation day for many green cowboys who did not earn their last set of spurs until they had faced the devil in his own den, so to speak, and lived to tell the story.

The year's work began in April when the general roundup began. Then some cowboys trailed the cattle to market in June, while the others remained on the ranch and tended to small jobs, such as rounding up and branding strays that had escaped the spring gathering. Most of the fall was devoted to gathering cattle for market and branding any further strays located in neighboring pastures. Even less work was done during the winter months. The cowboys simply supervised the stock and prepared for the next spring roundup.

As the nature of ranching changed, the cowboy faced many new chores—working on the feed farm, fixing fence, hauling hay, and, for punchers on Texas' Spur Ranch, working on an experimental farm. Some readily adapted to the new tasks. Others rebelled and moved to another ranch where they could cowboy. The cowboy is the "knight of the Plains," the dashing young man on horseback. He performed his daily work on horseback, he grew to know his horse. The Aztec warriors' impression that the Spanish rider and horse were part of the same animal might have been more nearly true of the cowboy. "I began to realize for the first time how well-founded the statement is that a cowboy lives on horseback," wrote Leon Noel, a New Yorker, after visiting cowboys on a New Mexico ranch. "You hardly ever see them walk." In addition, genuine cowboys wanted work on ranches that handled cattle. They did not want to be burdened with other ranch chores. The cowboy did not want to dismount to pitch a bale of hay.

The first major event of the cowboy's work calendar was the spring roundup. When the grass began to green and the vaqueros of New

Opening pages: Working
cattle in corral on foot.
Most modern ranch ropes
are medium lay (stiffness)
nylon, average 35 feet
in length. (Buckaroos
like c. 50 feet.) Original
reatas were braided
rawhide up to 80 feet long.
They required delicate
touch, are rare today.
"Grass ropes" of Manila
hemp followed, but
got limp in hot weather,
unmanageable in cold.
Above: Rider ropes
skittish colt in 06 corral.

Open-range branding in Texas, 1867, with mirage in background. Inaccuracies are odd stance of brander and impossibility of bringing a cow to its knees by one-handed pull on slack.

Mexico donned their summer sombreros, seasonal employees gathered their accoutrements and headed to the big ranches in hope of getting a job. The roundup on the Maxwell Land Grant Company range was one of the most colorful events of the year. "We reached camp at six o'clock, and received a pleasant welcome from old Uncle Sam, the cook," wrote Noel. "Soon after, the rest of the 'outfit,' six cowboys, came straggling in. . . .

"About nine o'clock we retired, I rolled myself up in my blankets under a tent between two of the cowboys. The next morning at five we had our breakfast, which by way of variation consisted of coffee with potatoes and beef—for dinner we had beef and potatoes with coffee. We were somewhat stiff after our ride of the previous day, and were delighted to hear that the cattle would be branded in a little cañon within five minutes walk of the camp."

One of the first jobs a roundup crew faced was breaking horses, should their remuda not be ready for the saddle. While Noel and his friends waited on the cowmen who had stock to sell, they occupied themselves riding the semiwild horses. A young cowboy named Van prepared to ride one of the roughest horses. "It took two men all of fifteen minutes to put the saddle on," recalled Noel. They attached the buck strap, then tied the stirrups together under the horse's belly, so they would not flap wildly at the animal's sides when he began his defense. They first let the horse try to buck off the saddle, thinking this would teach him the uselessness of resistance. "How that animal did jump, rear, and kick!" exclaimed Noel. "Now I understood why the boys had started him going without a rider on his back."

When the horse stopped for breath, Van jumped into the saddle. The horse that had two days before pitched a more talented rider than Van into the dust, breaking his collarbone and two ribs, sat still. But Van knew it would not last. Two riders already had mounted their horses, preparing to ride alongside to assist in guiding the bronco. "Pick out a soft spot, old fellow," shouted a cowboy, as the wild horse finally realized there was a man in the saddle and accepted the challenge. As in most instances, the cowboy won. The horse exhaustedly yielded, ready to play his part in the annual spring roundup.

Some cowboys made a living breaking broncos. When he could get no other kind of cowboying job, James McCauley took on an entire remuda of wild horses. "I was a long way from home and busted," he explained. "I told them to trot them out. The first one I tried was about as bad as any I ever tried in all my days. To tell the truth, he had me throwed. He pitched so hard and so high and so much that I give out, turned blind. Both my feet went out of the stirrups. But luck come to my rescue. He stopped to get his breath, and I got mine and got my feet in the stirrups and was ready for him when he started again. I found out that the horse was nine years old and had been rode at for about four years, two to six times a year. I never was so sore in all my days. They told me I had rode the worst one on the ranch and I need not dread the balance. Well, I rode something like forty of them. I tore my saddle completely up and all the clothes I had too, but I had learned to be a bronco buster. When I got done with that bunch of broncoes I was full of that job."

On another occasion, the boys pointed McCauley toward a big gray horse that he suspected of being an outlaw. "Nevertheless, I got one of them to hold him for me. All of them began to ask me what word must they send to my folks and if I had good life insurance and who of them was to get that new saddle when it come and what must they write to my girl. But while this was all being said I crawled up in the middle of him, told them to turn him loose. I had a big old quirt. Before he had time to move I gave him a rap down between the eyes that was kindly new to him, but, anyhow, he bogged his head and round he went. I was in a corral. He pitched around the thing twice. I hit him every time he hit the ground. Oh, but he did rag. He bawled a few times but I just kept on with the quirt. I could hear them asking each other where I was from. . . . 'But say, can't that kid put the quirt to them.'"

Cowboy-author S. S. Metzger wrote knowledgeably of the roundup and branding, describing the procedures that are still used on large ranches today. "Jack" Elliott, a "true American pioneer" and owner of the Bar X Ranch, was the wagon boss. "Reese, the best roper in the 'outfit,' . . . stood in the small entrance to the 'cavy' twirling his rope; and as each puncher designated the pony he intended riding that morning, Reese unerringly cast his lasso over its head and pulled it forth. All of the horses in the 'cavvy' were somewhat excited, but as each one felt the noose tighten about its neck it immediately quieted down and came calmly forth. Each man in turn removed the lariat from his horse, put the reins of the bridle around its neck, put on the bridle, dropped the reins to the ground, for the horse had been trained to stand when this was done, smoothed the saddle blankets upon its back, swung the heavy Mexican saddle into place, cinched it easily and then walked back to the fire for orders.

"'Jack' Elliott was issuing them. 'I an' Tom an' Ivan an' Sprint will cover Big Simpson this morning; the cattle is heavy that a-way,' he drawled, continuing in like manner until each puncher knew in what region he was to look for cattle, while riding the morning 'circle.'

"'Albert, you tell the boys over with the herd to work it right along now to the big draw on the Little Bend, near Warner's sheep camp. There's fine feedin' there an' water, an' git them there before it's hot. Chippie, you git the horses right along fer we'll sure need them. An', Wes, you have the grub-wagon at the water-hole, jes' by the willows, and grub fer them that eats. Well, boys, let's sasshay along now.'"

The cowboys scattered, driving balky cattle out of brush,

Wrangler on Bells brings
in remuda. Horses are held
in rope corral—a simple
arrangement of stakes and
one length of rope which
can be set up anywhere.
Horses tend to stand
in circle, facing outward,
so individuals are
easily roped for
cowboys by wagon boss.
Below: Cowboy with mount.

searching for them in box canyons. Metzger and twenty other cowboys were participating in probably the last cooperative roundup in Wyoming. Hands from eight ranches in southeastern Wyoming had gathered to catch the new-born calves and the yearlings that had eluded them the previous spring.

"We continued our work until the sun beat upon us without mercy," wrote Metzger. "One would always keep the herd moving towards the location of the noon camp while the other would ride to the nearby draws to look for cattle. Before noon, grimy with sweat and dust, we brought our cattle into camp and turned them into the main herd. As we approached the grub-wagon, from which stretched a fly of tarpaulin that told of shade and relief . . . three other punchers who had recently arrived in camp with Smitty from the 3J3 'outfit' [were] on hand to aid us in 'cutting out' their stock and branding it that afternoon. The four of them had been to a dance the night before at the Oasis, where, true to their nature, they had whirled the entire darkness through with a hay-rack load of damsels from the Cheyenne Laundry. At daybreak dancing ceased, whereupon they had mounted their ponies and trailed off through the sagebrush to work, while the young ladies had been driven in their conveyance back to the city to resume their vocation, at seven o'clock, somewhat the worse for wear.

"From time to time the punchers returned from the 'circle,' bringing in with them more cattle to be added to the main herd, which now numbered over four thousand. It was hot where we sat, even with the shade of the tarpaulin to protect us, and the flies buzzed incessantly. Smitty, squatted tailor fashion before us, kept humming drowsily,

Oh waltz me around ag'in El'ner,
Oh waltz me around on the schoolhouse floor.

"Slower and slower he droned it, very much in tune with the buzzing of the flies, until his head sank wearily upon his chest and he fell asleep. Chippie, the day horse wrangler, was bringing up the fresh mounts when Jack Elliot pushed Smitty over, awakening him with a start. 'Come on, boys, an' we'll get this yer cuttin' an' brandin' done before night,' he said; adding to Smitty, 'so this yearlin' can get his beauty sleep.'"

Jack Elliott let his cowboys catch their breath and finish their dinner, then he pushed them back onto the range, for much remained to be done before they bedded down for the night. "Over with the herd, much

Good cutting horse guides cull (animal that will not be sold) away from herd. Shoe Bar, 1909. Right: Hell for leather.

was going on. Four punchers were holding the constantly moving cattle, while four others were riding through them 'cutting out' the cows and calves of the 3J3 'outfit' . . . . Not far from them the branding fire was being prepared, for Wes and Clayton were gathering 'Kansas coal' in gunny sacks to be used as fuel. It was an intensely busy scene. Quietly a rider would turn his pony into the big herd, mark a cow, work her with her calf out of the herd, turn them over to a puncher, who drove them to the 'cut,' and returning, repeat the operation. By mid-afternoon 'the cut' had been made and we all assembled around the branding fire.

Breaking a bronco, Matador, 1908.

"Immediately the ropers began their work. Spotting an unbranded calf, they cast their lassos, catching it preferably by a hind leg, and dragging it with their horses, brought it to us by the branding fire. As it came near, one of us would grab it, reach over its back with both arms, seize it under the throat and hind leg, give it a lift so as to swing its legs off the ground and forward and then drop upon it. We were all careful to stick our right knee into its neck, and with an arm, double up and raise its upper front leg as far as possible. The calf was now helpless, except for its hind legs. These were cared for by another puncher, who grabbed the upper one as he sat down behind the calf and pulled it towards him as he pushed against the lower one with both feet. Then a third puncher rushed up with the red-hot branding irons. We had always thrown the calves upon the right side and now the new arrival sizzled the 3J3 marks into the left side, always at the same place, while the calves bawled and struggled. They were careful not to burn deeper than through the hair and into the epidermis, so as to kill the roots of the former, for a bad burn meant fly blow and disease to the stock. At the same time Smitty dexterously handled the knife. First he would 'dulap' each one in the middle of the throat. This was accomplished by slitting a piece of the hide, about three inches long, upward along the throat, so that as it hung, it showed plainly from a distance to the eyes of the cattle world gazing from either side, that this was a 3J3 head of stock. Then the left ear was cut, a small right-angular piece being taken out of its outside edge, known as the 'ear-mark'; and behold, the calf would ever afterwards present to the puncher, who approached from the front or rear, ample evidence of its ownership. All of the bull calves were cut and as each was finished it was turned loose, little the worse for wear, as they generally would return to their mothers and begin feeding. They ranged in age from a few days to 'yearlings,' each equally hardy and the latter most difficult to handle, as their strength surpassed ours individually, and when thrown their stubby horns would bruise one considerably unless the puncher was a master of the art."

By six o'clock the cowboys had finished the day's work, and they headed back to camp at a "mad gallop," each man nursing a healthy appetite. Camp, of course, had been moved again, this time to the top of a hill where they could catch the cool evening breeze that blew the mosquitos away. Metzger paused to enjoy the scenery: "The sun was now casting shadows of blues and purples through the draws and over the crevices in the bluffs. (Remington always pictured them so accurately.) For a mile behind us we could see the herd grazing, with the punchers watching it. They were herding

151

it more closely for the night. Slowly they worked turning back the cows first at one point and then at another. It was a restful and peaceful scene." After supper the punchers sat in the "long twilight of soft and bizarre colors," rolled their cigarettes and smoked and chatted. It was here that much of the oral tradition of the range was passed on. They talked of the old days, the long Texas trail, "stories of an age before most of us were born."

Then they fell asleep one by one. Metzger lay awake, gazing for some time into the heavens, but the sweet, cool night air soon worked its charm and he slept soundly until he was awakened to stand his turn at watch. Three of them were to herd the cattle for the next two hours, the last watch of the night. "The night-herd work is always apportioned equally among the men," Metzger pointed out. "Each set rides night-guard two hours each night. The first night out the sets, and the time for them to ride, are given out by the 'boss' or foreman of the 'outfit.' The following night the sets take the watch succeeding the one they were first given, and so on during the round-up, so there can be no favoritism and no criticism. None are exempted from this work.

"We quietly rode to the herd, relieving the three men on guard and continued at equal distances apart to ride around it. The moon had gone down, yet we could still distinguish objects near by, and the herd lay beside us as a dark mass. The cattle were quiet, so Jack joined me and we rode together in silence. I rolled a cigarette, struck a match and lit it."

Metzger and his companions continued their conversation. "I've seen cattle stampede fer less than that," said Jack, an old-timer who had been up the trail several times. "Once they git a-millin' they is liable to go fer most nothin'. One cant back them heavy then as to their notions. We was a-comin' up on the Old Trail once when we hog-tied a new puncher, as we was short. He sure eluciadated us on the moods of cows, right off, so none of the boys was particularly p'lite t' him. Then it come along one night when it was sure black an' awesome lookin' an' the foreman he puts this yer yearlin' on the same jingle as we is a-ridin'. We was just a-settin' contented like in our slumbers when we heard him break out in imitation of the nightingale, which said warbler no sooner trailed into them scrub long-horns than they ups an' was a doin', an' doin' damn rapid-like. Nacherally they stampedes, none a-blaiming them whatsoever, an' we ups an' sasshays about an' trails after them until sun-up. That ride aint no sport, let me enlighten you. Bud Kimball rounds up with a broken leg and we was plumb fortunate to escape that a-way. Next day we rounds them up an' herds them into camp an' finds our young prodigy there a-waitin' to be rescued, he's that lost. 'Whatever did you warble fer?' I says to this party. 'Because I read it in books,' he says back to me. An' we was a-advertisin' fer a new puncher next what wasn't so familiar with eddication.'"

Jack talked on until he came to the present settlement in Wyoming. Real-estate agents in northern Colorado and southern Wyoming were advertising cheap land and attracting large numbers of buyers. "I kin recollect away back in the old days in Nebrasky. I was jes' a yearlin' then, like these yer boys with our outfit. An' like yearlin's I was plumb full of health an'

155

ZX buckaroos roping an ornery cow. Below: Tailing a calf down after heading & heeling. Bottom: Doctoring a bull.

Top: Padlock branding
crew. Bottom: The
brand, freshly burned.
Following pages: Heading
& heeling on Quien
Sabe. Pages 164-5: Cow
is roped, thrown,
injected, and released
(with cowboy ready to ride
her a bit for fun).

hell an' belivin', same as these boys, that cattle punchin' was the one big show on earth, when along comes them settlers jes' like these yer. Only they was a whole lot poorer an' more in need of grub-stakin' than a band o' coyotes after an easy winter. We sure ridiculed an' called them suckers, same as these boys is doin' now, but they has clean pushed us off that State an' owns it all now. It was jes' as dry an' desolate-like lookin' there then as it is here now, an' I calculates these yer suckers is a stampedin' this a-way now an' we aint got long fer to saddle up an' rustle out. They is bound fer developin', improvin' an' howlin' successes. They'll git it all all right, but as fer me I don't know nothin' but cattle an' this here air an' these yer plains an' their freedom an' all hits me where I live an' I'm roped, hog-tied an' branded ferever to them."

As the sun began to show over the eastern horizon, Metzger ended the conversation, rode over to the chuck wagon and roused the cook, who jumped up and began preparing breakfast. Another day of hard work had begun.

There were, of course, many other phases to the cowboy's work. One of the prestige jobs for any puncher was "rep," the man who represented his ranch at the neighborhood roundups to be sure that the boss got all his cattle back. Mat Jones remembered repping for Bud Powers as one of his first jobs. Trying to keep up with the older hands and prove his worth, Jones quickly got into a quarrel with another cowboy about a steer. Although the steer bore the 2P brand belonging to Powers, the other puncher insisted that a brand that had been marked out was the legal brand, and that the cow therefore belonged to him. Not wanting a confrontation, Jones gathered up his cattle and left before the scheduled departure, taking the disputed steer with him, a victory over an older cowhand that he did not soon forget.

Teddy Blue Abbott found repping more complex than he had hoped. "I had been hungry and thirsty myself plenty of times," he related, "but all the rest was a picnic compared to one time in the summer of '82, in the Nebraska sand hills. After I went to work for the Olive outfit . . . this other fellow and I were sent out with a string of eight horses apiece to rep with Bill Cody's outfit on the roundup. They told us they would be camped on a certain lake in the sand hills, and we was to join them there. So we rode all one day, about forty miles, but when we got to the place they were supposed to be, they weren't there and the lake was dry." It was a misunderstanding, but Teddy and his friends had gone astray and were in trouble.

"We hadn't brought no grub. We expected to find the outfit, and cowboys don't carry box lunches. So we made camp that night without food or water. Next morning we started out again, expecting to find them at another lake we knew about, that was another day's ride away. It was just like the day before, only that much worse. No water and nothing to eat. We couldn't even kill a jack rabbit. There was no game in there except antelope —and we couldn't get close enough to those to get a shot at them. The first day you want a drink awful bad. The second day you can't think of nothing else—can't talk—can't spit. You just got to keep going, and you rope a fresh horse every couple of hours, and you go along at a high trot, pounding that saddle.

Breaking a mustang in California
picket-fence corral. 1874.

"About five or six o'clock at night we found this other little lake we were looking for, and there was some water in it. About six inches deep, swimming with polliwogs, and coffee-colored with alkali. We strained out the polliwogs through a handkerchief and tried to drink it. The alkali was so strong we couldn't keep it on our stomachs. The horses got a drink, though, and we stripped our clothes off and rolled around in it, and washed our faces, and that helped some. There was a lot of tule weeds around there, and while we was taking off the pack, I saw a coyote sneak out of the other side of the tule weeds and hit a lope for the hills. The other fellow took a shot at him and knocked him over. We each took a hind quarter of that coyote, and we got some cow chips and made a fire and roasted it. It smelled like carrion. I would take a bite and then retch, and after a while I got just one swallow down.

"We made our beds and went to sleep, figuring that we could make it to the Platte River next day, fifty or sixty miles, and get out of this alive if somewhat thinner. But at daylight we heard a bell ringing and it woke us up. And a fellow rode up on horseback and wanted to know what the hell we was doing there. When we told him, I thought he'd die laughing. He was out after the horses for the roundup, and he had seen ours and come down there, thinking they were some of his.

"They were camped half a mile over the hill, on a bubbling spring."

One of the most dangerous duties, because of the possibility of stampede, was the night guard, which all punchers shared. "The first night I stood guard I'll never forget," wrote McCauley. The cattle were driven close together and held in a group throughout the night, so none would be lost. "About dark they will all . . . lay down," continued McCauley. "And then everybody goes to the wagon, which is usually camped close, but about two or three. These cowboys are called the first guard. They will hold the cattle there part of the night and then they will wake up two or three more and they will stand their part, and so on. I was put on first guard until 10:30 o'clock. I didn't have any trouble with the cattle, as they lay all right, but I didn't think my guard would ever be out, the time dragged so awful slow. But finely the second guard took them and I turned in. The next morning was a fine day and

we was moving on towards Montana, slowly.

"On the third night, as usual, I was on the first guard, just Scandlous John and me, and about nine o'clock a black cloud from the northwest came up. I had on my slicker, or oil coat. It began to rain in torrents. The vivid lightning began to flash. The thunder began to roar. And all at once the steers got on their feet and in less time than it takes to tell it they was gone. The night was as dark as ink, only for the lightning. My horse was on his job, so he stayed with the cattle. Then I realized that the so much talked of stampeding herd of longhorn steers was now a reality. Every time it would lighten and a loud clap of thunder follow they would change their course, and in a short time I found the herd had split or divided, but into how many bunches I didn't know. After some two hours of storm the rain quit and soon it cleared off and the moon shined out, but I didn't know where my pard was or which way the wagon might be.

"I had about three hundred head of steers and after everything was still they lay down and I thought I'd see if I could find the other part of the herd. But to my sorrow I could not, so I thought I'd shoot my six-shooter and see if anybody would come or answer me. Bang she went and away went the bunch I was holding. Now I had more trouble than if I had a let things alone. After chasing them for an hour, I guess, I got them stopped, but I didn't shoot any more. I saw I was in to it for the night and so I made the best of a bad bargain. Well, the moon in all its beauty came up at last and as the sun arose across the eastern horizon in all its glory they never was a pore, wore out sleepier boy than I was. But still I was in trouble, for there I was with a bunch of cattle all alone with nobody in sight and I didn't know which way to go in the wagon. I was so hungry and tired I didn't know what to do.

"About ten o'clock a man came in sight. They was looking for me but didn't know which way to look. He told me the direction the wagon was. I lit out. I had drifted something like ten miles to the southeast and if any boy ever did enjoy something to eat it was me. If bacon and beans ever tasted good it was then. The boys all told the boss he had lost his tenderfoot, but when they found out I had held a bunch all night they didn't say tenderfoot any more. I thought 'twas the most miserable night I had ever experienced in all my life. They said it was the way they initiated all the down east boys, so I took

Calves may endure branding, ear marking, dehorning, castration, and inoculation in series of fast actions requiring perhaps two seven-man crews on ground and several teams of mounted ropers. These pictures were taken at Bell Ranch.

Catching calf, heating irons, branding and dehorning. Branding is essential identification. Cattle do mingle on range and rustling does occur. In cowboy lingo, a fellow puncher is said to be "working for same iron." Following pages: Cowboys on foot are giving rider some slack so he can re-cinch loose saddle.

it for granted and hoped 'twoud not happen any more. Things rocked on very well till we struck the Arkansaw River between La Junta and Pueblo, Colorado. It got so stormy up there in the breaks of the Rocky Mountains that we had a storm every night, nearly. . . .

"My real troubles was yet to come. When we reached the Arkansaw River we went up it three or four days before we crossed. When finely we put into it, it was about level full, as the snow had been melting up in the mountains long enough to swell it until it was a raging torrent. I waited as long as I could before I went in. I didn't get in good until it was swimming. I didn't get far before my horse got tangled in some drift and sank to rise no more. I had taken off my boots and most of my clothes for fear of something like this. The first thing that come handy was a four year old steer. I got him by the tail and away we went for the other side, which we reached after so long a time. I promised myself I'd never swim the Arkansaw any more.

"I had lost my saddle, bridle, blankets and spurs and was broke; that is, I didn't have enough money to buy a new outfit. What to do I didn't know, but I kept my troubles to myself, and the boys began to guy me about riding bareback until Scandlous John came to my rescue. He told me to ride on the chuck wagon until he could buy me a new outfit. I felt some better. In the course of a week he sent to Pueblo and got me a new outfit out and out. Then I was one of the boys—a new $45 saddle. But I promised myself that I'd never go up the trail with a herd any more, that swimming them rivers was just a little bit too dangerous for me.

"Finally we came to the last river. It was the worst of them all, and I would not have tried to swim it for all the cattle up there. 'Tis noted for its swiftness and it has two currents. The top current is some two feet deep, and the under current runs twice as fast as the top. 'Twas the noted Yellowstone River. When you go below the top current nothing comes up. 'Tis such a suck to it that to sink in the Yellowstone is a gone fawn skin. When we got there, the other two herds had not crossed. They seemed to be waiting for us. We crossed close to Miles City. There is some islands there. We would put the cattle in and some men there with boats helped us swim them to an island. From it we would swim them for the next island.

"After all five of the herds got there about half of the men quit and went to Miles City and blowed in their money. From there on we put all the cattle in one herd and just drifted them on to the ranch, which was not very far. We could not drive so many cattle. All we could do was just drift them through. We was fourteen days crossing the five herds."

"With the loading of the cattle came the 'paying off' and the cow-boy's brief vacation before returning to another year's round of hard work and coarse fare," noted Charles Moreau Harger for **Scribner's Magazine.** "It was not, perhaps, to be expected that after a nearly twelve-month of life on the prairies he should spend his outing in quiet and dignity. And seldom indeed did he. The cattle towns catered to his worst passions, and saloons and dance-houses flourished with startling exuberance. Gambling ran riot, and quarrels ending in murder were of frequent occurrence. During the height of the season might was the only law. . . ."

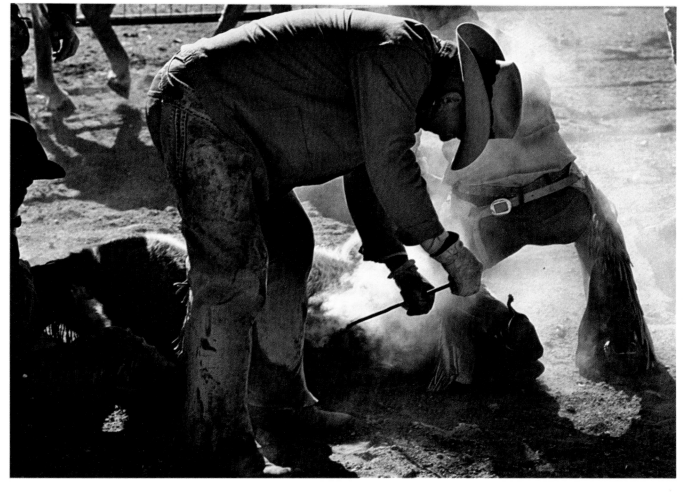

Preceding pages: Spraying
cattle on 06's. Opposite:
Dipping at Four Sixes.
Left & below: Castration
and branding at Padlock.

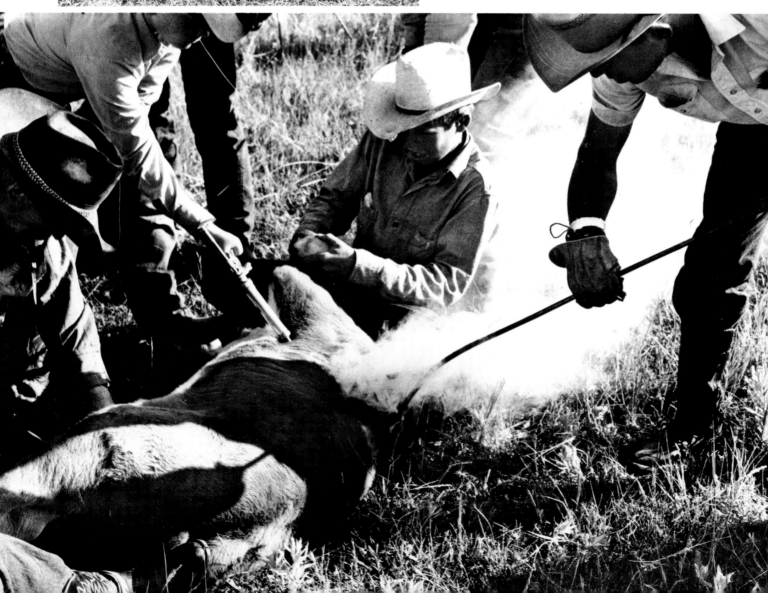

New Mexico ranch of 1874 brands its
cattle inside stone corral.

After the spring roundup, the pace slacked. "During the
summer months," wrote Noel, the cowboy's "work consists in herding the
cattle, rounding them up, branding the calves and breaking in their saddle
horses. In winter there is not so much to be done. The outfit then goes into a
permanent camp, living in a cabin made of logs, having the interstices filled
with stones, plastered together with mud. From this camp they circle round
through the country, bringing in the weak and sickly cattle, which they fear
might otherwise not survive the winter storms, feeding them hay and alfalfa
until they have recovered. Many cattlemen simply let their herds run the
whole winter without care, but it pays to give them some little attention."
McCauley recalled that he "laid around all summer, only the pasture to ride
and my broncs. About the first of August I rode over to the St. Louis Ranch,
took my mount and went to the L-Z Ranch, as they wanted to send a man. We
got over there a week ahead of the work. We didn't want to go back. They had
plenty of watermelons and grapes to feed all on the [Blanco] Canyon. We took
in two dances in that week and had a good, high-heeled time. We worked
some two weeks."

Not all the hands worked during the winter, simply be-
cause there was not enough to keep them all busy. Bob Kennon recalled how
fortunate he was to have year round employment. "We were all . . . at headquarters wondering if we'd be retained or paid off," he said. "We'd go over to
the office one following the other, as Bill [Murphy, the boss] sent for us.
When he had finished business with one hand, he would send for another,

178

until all were accounted for, kept on or turned off. I must have been about the twelfth one to be called to the office.

"'Do you have any money?' Bill asked me.

"'Yes, sir. I have the wages I've earned,' I answered.

"'What have you planned on doing this winter?' he asked.

"I told him I'd arranged to wash dishes in a restaurant in Miles City for my room and board.

"'Would you like to work here at the ranch this winter?' he asked.

"I told him I sure would and he hired me for the winter, and I went back to send another hand to his office. . . .

"I tended sheep camps, herded sheep at various times while herders went off on sprees, and hauled hay to cattle. I didn't stay at the big bunkhouse, for Mike Klein, who looked after the studs and jacks, asked me to stay with him, as he got lonesome out at his house. Mike's place was across Big Coulee Creek, about a quarter-mile south of the big ranch house. He sure loved a nice house with carpets on the floor. He always took his overshoes, or soiled shoes, off on the porch, putting on carpet slippers to wear indoors. He even had a piano, which he could play."

During the off-season the cowboys made sure their horses were well shod. Horses were not usually shod in much of the Southwest unless they became tenderfooted, then the shoes were left on until the condition improved. In the rocky ground of New Mexico, however, horses had to be shod. "Each rider was responsible for the condition of his string of horses," according to Mat Jones. "When one of them became tenderfooted, he had to shoe his horse. A keg of shoes of assorted sizes was kept in the chuck wagon along with the proper tool.

"When a horse needed shoeing, that evening the rider would get the hammer, rasp, and pincers from the wagon, select either a size zero or size one for that particular horse, and do the job. Size two shoes were kept in the keg for the larger horses. As cowboy horseshoes were made of wrought iron, the shoe could be shaped to fit the hoof without being heated. For this, the shoe was laid over a convenient rock, the head of an ax, or anything suitable for pounding the shoe into the proper shape for each hoof.

"Some of the boys were better at shoeing than others, and the handiest man would take care of that job for the chuck wagon teams. I never became adept at shoeing. Therefore I always made friends with someone who was and then traded work with him, doing something in return that he could not do so well."

Frank Collinson, a Texas rancher of considerable experience and reputation, pointed out that much of the cowboy's work involved things not a part of the normal routine. "Prairie fires have always been terrifying," he recalled. "Whether caused by a bolt of lightning or spread by the careless flip of a match or cigarette butt, they have brought fear to man since the beginning of time. The red man knew their danger on the Plains of Texas, as did the buffalo hunter and pioneer cowman. . . . The ranchman continues to dread the prairie fire. He is constantly on guard against it, especially during

long dry spells. He knows how quickly it can ruin a range and leave only charred and blackened debris in its wake.

"When I managed the Jingle Bob cattle I hired a man with a plow to turn up a fireguard from Duck Creek to the Cottonwood Mott, South Pease River. This was the first fireguard ever cut around a ranch upon the Plains.

"I have seen and heard of many prairie fires in my day. Some of them were so devastating and covered so many miles that they are still talked about in that part of the country. Among them was a fire on the Matador in 1907.

"That fire, like many others, started when a cowboy carelessly flipped a cigarette butt into the dry grass near Petersburg. The flame was soon whipped into a roaring giant, as the wind was blowing sixty miles an hour from the west. There were few people living on the Plains at that time, and it was impossible to get enough fire fighters to put it out. It burned a strip sixty miles long, jumped Blanco Canyon, and came east to the Cap Rock. Just as it was about to jump off the Cap Rock, the wind turned to the north and made a lead fire out of the south-side fire for a distance of twenty-five miles. This fire wiped out all of the grass between the Cap Rock and Blanco Canyon, a distance in length of thirty-five or forty miles. The cowboys on the ranch fought the east-side fire for two days and nights before they got it out. Luckily the wind did not change again. Had it switched to the west, it would have wiped out the entire south portion of the Matador range. Only a gentle breeze blew out of the north, giving the cowboys time to whip out the entire east-side fire.

"The cowboys fought the fire with sacks, saddle blankets, jackets, warehouse brooms, or anything else they could find that would beat out the flames. One of the most successful methods of fighting a fire was to kill a beef and cut it partly open. A rope was tied to a hind foot and forefoot, and the carcass was pulled over the fire by the cowboys on horseback. The bloody organs from the animal's stomach would put out the fire. A carcass could be used for four or five hours quite successfully.

"Luckily the buffalo grass in Texas was mostly short. If the wind was right, it burned fast and did not result in the terrifying experiences suffered in the country north of the Canadian River where the grass was long."

Prairie fires only complicated the already difficult task facing the cowboy. From a youth who only knew how to rope and ride, the cowboy had developed into a talented, skilled worker who built and fixed fence, blacksmithed, wrangled horses, trailed, branded, and doctored cattle, and performed countless other tasks that continually developed on a ranch. As they neared the end of another year's labor, perhaps they shared Frank Collinson's thoughts as he recalled the first trail drive to the Northwest. "I think of the hardships we experienced [and] I wonder if there was really much glamour or adventure to the trip," he mused. "It was 98 per cent hard work, but I am glad I had the experience . . . we helped make cattle history on that drive."

7

the decline of open-range ranching

Although the cattle industry created millionaires, changed the nation's eating habits, and generated America's first hero figure, the heyday of ranching lasted less than a generation. Cattlemen who knew that a serious blizzard would kill weak stock and considered a five to ten percent loss each winter normal were astonished at the losses in Kansas, Colorado, and the Texas Panhandle during the unusually severe winter of 1885-86. Thousands of cattle were frozen or so weakened by the cold that they fell victim to predators. Several leading cattlemen urged that ranchers generally change their manner of operating, but few were seriously concerned and sometimes the advice was off the mark. "Too much stress cannot be placed on the importance of handling the cattle quietly and carefully," the president of the Lincoln County Live Stock Association told his membership. Gather the "cattle in small bunches, take plenty of time, see that all work is done satisfactorily, and allow no gambling in camp."

Gambling or the manner of handling cattle were not the main problems cattlemen faced. An overstocked range and hope of getting high prices for the beeves were the real problems. Viewing the disaster in the Midwest, several cattlemen realized that the situation in Montana, Wyoming, and the Dakotas was potentially worse because the winters were more severe. When 1886 proved to be a dry summer, grass suffered and the cattle fed inadequately. "All over the territory the same cry has gone up," reported the Helena (Montana) **Independent.** "The grass on the ranges grew but slimly and cured before its time for lack of moisture . . . Much depends upon the coming winter." In addition, several cattlemen had bought some eastern cattle that showed an amazing proclivity: They waited to be fed rather than foraging with the native stock.

Hoping to avert disaster on their own range, some Montanans began searching for solutions. At least one ranch paper urged them to sell. "Beef is low, very low, and prices are tending downward, while the market continues to grow weaker every day," warned the **Rocky Mountain Husbandman.** "But for all that, it would be better to sell at a low figure, than to endanger the whole herd by having the range overstocked."

In reality, only the fortunate ones managed to sell. Some cattlemen moved their herds to Canada's open range. By September, 1886, more than 250,000 head were north of the border. Others let small ranchers feed their cattle on the "shares," that is, they shared the sale price of the cow, but such desperate measures had no real effect on the overcrowding.

Snow began to fall in November. "The storm . . . in this locality was, in many respects, the worst on record," reported the Bismarck **Daily Tribune.** "The snow drifted to a greater extent than ever before and it penetrated buildings wherever it was possible for wind to find its way." Cattlemen realized that only a chinook (warm spell) could save their herds and dared hope for one when the temperature rose dramatically around mid-December. Then the worst blizzard in Montana's recorded history hit in January. Cowboys could not leave the bunkhouse for weeks and snow and ice covered the grass. Cattle roamed about the range, even entering towns search-

Opening pages: Scott
McKinley cowboys with his
dog in Montana snow
during fall roundup, John
Scott Cattle Co. Dogs
often are excellent
herders, particularly in
getting cows out of brush.

ing for food. Cowmen watched helplessly from their ranch house windows as the skinny, half-frozen beeves poked hopelessly at the crust covering the ground. Thousands of cattle starved. The blizzard produced one of Charlie Russell's most famous pictures. Spending the winter on the L. E. Kaufman ranch, Russell drew a picture to tell Kaufman the condition of his stock. Thinking that perhaps humor would ease the bad news, Russell painted "Waiting for A Chinook," a caricature of a cow with her ribs showing and eyes almost closed being circled by a band of wolves. The picture has become almost the symbol of the Montana disaster of 1886-87.

Teddy Blue Abbott was in the middle of the storm working for Granville Stuart. "I wore two pairs of wool socks, a pair of moccasins, a pair of Dutch socks that came up to the knees, a pair of government over-shoes, two suits of heavy underwear, pants, overalls, chaps, and a big heavy shirt," he said. "I got a pair of woman's stockings and cut the feet out and made sleeves. I wore wool gloves, and a great big sealskin cap. That way I kept warm enough. But not any too warm."

Thousands of cattle were saved only because cowpunchers were willing to get out in sixty-degree-below-zero weather and move them to forage. Cattle fell in air holes in the frozen rivers. They froze standing up. The cowboys "worked like slaves," said Teddy. "They saved thousands of cattle," but "untold thousands went down. . . ."

Teddy himself was almost trapped in the blizzard while returning from a Christmas visit with some friends. "When we got over the hill and the wind and snow hit us so hard we could not see fifty feet ahead or hardly breathe," he recalled. "We tried to make Tucker's cabin again but missed it. That night we rode into a narrow canyon where we were out of the wind, but we got off our horses in snow up to our waist. We built a fire and made coffee, and held our meat on sticks until it thawed out, and ate it hot and raw. We never took the bridles off the horses, because there was nothing for them to eat. Next morning we lit out for home and it was a fight for life. We had to ride sideways to the wind. . . . The wind blew the breath right out of our bodies and the snow cut like a knife." Finally, Teddy and his friend made it back to the ranch. When they started to unpack their horses they found the ropes frozen and their fingers so stiff they could hardly untie them.

The long-hoped-for Chinook finally arrived around the first of March. "At the close of one hundred days of the severest winter weather that this region has ever known the warm wind bared the hills, settled the snow on the prairies, and in places started the running water in the valleys . . .," reported the **Dakota Settler and Burleigh County Farmer** of Bismarck. The cowboys gradually emerged from their besieged cabins to inspect their losses, but they were difficult to assess. The **Yellowstone Journal** (Miles City) estimated that twenty-five percent of the cattle in Colorado, Wyoming, and Montana died. The Bismarck **Tribune** predicted that if the snow did clear up immediately the loss would approach seventy-five percent. Granville Stuart initially estimated his losses at ten percent, but later pointed out that "it was impossible to tell just what losses were for a long time as the cattle drifted in the big January storm. We did not get some of ours back for a

Above: Trailing Scott
herd over a ridge. Opposite:
Rounding up strays.
Note two in background.
Right: Many ranches now load
range cowboys' horses on
truck, drive them as close
to work area as possible.
Here Matador truck loads
horses for day's end
return to headquarters.

187

year. Our entire losses were sixty-six percent of the herd." One outfit on the Little Missouri River scrounged up only three of its cattle after a two-week roundup.

Unable to believe the extent of devastation, cattlemen hesitated to estimate their losses. "We had a perfect smashup all through the cattle country of the northwest," Teddy Roosevelt wrote his friend Henry Cabot Lodge. "The losses are crippling. For the first time I have been utterly unable to enjoy a visit to my ranch. I shall be glad to get home." "The returns of the winter losses dribbled in," wrote John Clay. "Men hoped against hope during the spring roundups, but the fall tallies told the ultimate story. . . . It was not the dead ones that were gone but the live ones that were left that told the tale." Stuart guessed the total loss to be near $20,000,000.

Many ranchers were ruined; more lost their enthusiasm. "A business that had been fascinating to me before, suddenly became distasteful," wrote Stuart. "I never wanted to own again an animal that I could not feed and shelter." Others were even more pessimistic. "The fact that we have now to face," commented one, "is that the range of the past is gone; that of the present is of little worth and cannot be relied on in the future." What happened to the Swan Land and Cattle Company was only representative of ranches all over the West. Thousands of Swan cattle died in the disaster, forcing the Scottish owners to investigate Swan and his entire operation. The ranch was soon in the hands of receivers. The Scots sadly realized that the book count was grossly overestimated and that 200 bulls, 2,200 steers, and 5,500 cows simply had to be written off. They replaced Swan with a Scot named Finlay Dunn, who rebuilt the company. Within two years Swan was a broken, poverty-stricken figure, but the Scots rescued the ranch and gradually turned it into a legitimate, moneymaking endeavor.

By now sober realism led foreign investors to realize that an inflated book count and a disastrous winter were only some of the calamities that could strike down profits. One rancher stood by in astonishment as udders blistered by sunlight reflected off the snow prevented his cows from suckling their calves. West Texas ranchers seemed to encounter new poisonous weeds in every pasture they opened, and cattle rustlers and Indians continued their costly antics. At least one foreigner professed to have the system figured out: "When the winter has been good, the summer has been bad. When the drought has been on its best behavior, the blizzard has been violent all over the plains. The one thing that has not varied has been the downward run of prices."

The failures and bankruptcies were too numerous and widespread to be blamed on the poor management and extravagance of a few foreign cattle barons. The entire industry was overcrowded and overextended. The disaster of 1886-87 and the ensuing hesitancy of financial institutions to extend money to such a depressed industry were more to blame. Without ready cash, ranchers could not recover from even a minor setback. In the Big Bend region of Texas, which later proved to be excellent cattle country, Frank Collinson went broke facing continual drought. He feared the potential of a ranch in the Big Bend but succumbed to the excitement and expectation. He appreciated the "pristine beauty" of the country and gloried in its unusual features. He floated down the Rio Grande until he came to the "Grand Canyon," Santa Elena Canyon. "I cast my eyes upward almost two thousand feet, to the top of the almost perpendicular walls of this scenic canyon, and noted that the rocks at its top looked as if they had been split apart. Some mighty giant could easily fit them together again. . . . We drank in the magnificent view, the finest I had seen during my sojourn in the Southwest. There were mountain ranges of the Big Bend, the Santiago, the Chisos." There were streams, wild bees, and wild life. And it was good cattle country.

Collinson moved to the Big Bend as half-owner of a ranch on Terlingua Creek, near the Rio Grande, in 1888. He soon realized that his initial apprehension had been correct. "In 1891 we suffered the worst drought I have ever known," he later recalled. "There was no rain for three years. Most of the cattle died or were driven out of the country. Several big ranches lost all of their stock. Some of the owners could not take it and committed suicide." Collinson also gave up on the country. "I faced such problems half of my life and concluded that the Big Bend is another Pharaoh's Dream—a few good years are followed by more lean years, which eat up all that the good years have made, and then some."

Old-time cowboy plays his fiddle, Three Block Ranch, NM, 1905-10.

With ranchers going broke, the trail drivers also suffered. They had been losing business for several years, because of the overstocked northern ranges, and because northerners trying to upgrade their breeds wanted no more Texas longhorns. From a high in 1884, the business dropped to dream-shattering lows in 1887. Ike T. Pryor apparently believed that any number of cattle could be handled in one drive. In 1884 he employed 165 cowboys and more than 1,000 horses to move 45,000 South Texas cattle northward in one single drive! The railroad and less purchasing in the north combined to decrease trail drives every year after that. From a high of 91,000 in 1884, the firm of Lytle, McDaniel, Schreiner, and Light shipped 40,000 cattle in 1885, 25,000 in 1886, and 12,000 in 1887, after the impact of the disastrous winter had begun to take effect. Lytle, McDaniel, and Light left the firm in the able hands of Charles Schreiner of Kerrville, Texas, who set out to salvage the company and pay the debts. John W. Light even sold his ranch and took a job as a cowboy on it.

Clear as it was to most observers that ranching had to change radically to survive, good weather following the winter disaster convinced several die-hards that the old method of open-range ranching was still viable. The unprecedented snows had left a tremendous amount of moisture in the mountains. Spring thaws brought rampaging streams and a beautiful stand of grass. The overgrazed land revived and there were fewer cattle to eat the grass. Some cattlemen even hoped to be able to return to the old practice of summer and winter ranges. At the same time an enormous Indian reservation in northern Montana was cut into three sections by the Bureau of Indian Affairs and reduced in size, rendering heretofore unavailable grazing land open to cattlemen. For a few brief moments it appeared that the old range ways might still work.

But the vision flickered for only a few months. The harsh

Throwing out coffee
dregs at log-house
line camp on an icy fall
day in Montana.

winter had wrecked the rancher. More than livestock had been lost. Confidence had been seriously undermined. The public lost interest in "cattle barons" and "bovine kings." Even those who had been strong advocates of the open range now turned against the practices and techniques that had made the disaster possible. "A man who turns out a lot of cattle on a barren plain without making provision for feeding them," warned the Cheyenne **Sun,** "will not only suffer a financial loss but also the loss of the respect of the community in which he lives."

Although some ranchers realized that they had overstocked their range and held onto the cattle even when it appeared that disaster approached, others attempted to find excuses. Sure targets of the blame were the foreigners who had behaved so extravagantly. "Of all the English snobs of great pretentions, who flew so high and sank so low, probably the Frewens are the chiefs," crowed the Cheyenne **Daily Sun.** "Their careers in Wyoming as cattle kings will long be remembered. They . . . made cowboys of freshly imported lads from England, maintained a princely establishment on the frontier, . . . established relay stations so as to make lightning journeys through the territory; had flowers shipped to the ranch, and conducted business . . . on a system . . . that was a constant surprise even to the most reckless and extravagant Americans. It is this method . . . that has brought an important and legitimate business into discredit in the East." Another observer was more blunt and pessimistic: "Range husbandry is over, is ruined, destroyed. It may have been by the insatiable greed of its followers."

There was sufficient publicity for the demise of open-range ranching that no one need have continued in ignorance. Outside capital was cut off and the cattlemen would never again be able to take such chances as earlier seemed routine. Those who remained in business found the profit margin so small that even a minor disaster in the coming winter would wipe them out. "It is extremely probable that the experience of the stockmen of Western Dakota and Montana this winter will bring about a radical change in the present system of stockraising," claimed the Bismarck **Weekly Tribune.** "This experience from the financial standpoint should teach stockmen to keep smaller herds and care for them well. . . ." Another journalist wrote off the losses to "carelessness," and urged "close-herding" of the stock during the coming year.

An article that appeared in the Great Falls **Tribune** in July, 1887, summed up the problems that were forcing the dramatic change in ranching. Prophetically entitled "The Last Drive," the article pointed out that some 50,000 cattle then on the trail from Texas to the northern states would "about-face" and head back to Texas. "There is absolutely no market for the cattle," observed the reporter, "and to turn the herds back is the only solution." Furthermore, continued the article, the ranges in the north could stand no more grazing stock. "The action is a most important one, inasmuch as it practically removes from existence forever the long-used cattle trail for the transportation of cattle."

The new era was properly begun when a correspondent for the **Northwestern Live Stock Journal** headlined a story in March, 1887, that the manager of one of the largest ranches on Powder River had arrived home with a shipment of 12,000 pounds of grass seed. The winter disaster had proved the folly of relying solely on range grass for forage. Ranchers now would have to have hay stored up for winter feed. "It was evident that the old system of the open range was passing and this was intensified by a series of dry years," recalled John Clay, manager of one of the largest ranches. "We therefore commenced to get quit of all frills and come down to earth, as the cowboys express it. We rented out our ranches . . . paying so much per ton for hay for every one put in the stack and then we paid the renters so much a month in winter time for feeding out the hay."

More ranchers turned to fencing, and those who had fences used them more extensively. Before 1874 fencing was quite a problem, because it had to be made of shrubs, rocks, or wood, all difficult to arrange in a fence and fairly easy to destroy. But after the Civil War, Joseph F. Glidden, a farmer in De Kalb, Illinois, convinced himself that a "barbed wire" fence could be made. In November, 1874, Glidden took out a patent, hired a crew, and began his Barb Fence Company. He sold all he could produce at eighteen cents a pound. Within a few months he had installed steam machinery and turned out five tons of barbed wire a day. Glidden sold half his patent to an eastern firm that had perfected a mechanical method of producing the wire, and more than 3,000,000 pounds of barbed wire were sold in 1876. The output jumped to the staggering total of more than 80,000,000 pounds in 1880, because Glidden had solved one of the real problems plaguing both farmers and ranchers—cheap fencing that was easy to construct, easy to maintain, and durable. The price of the fence, moreover, decreased because of improved production methods: from $20 a hundred pounds in 1870 to $4 in 1890. As the ranchers turned to fewer and better breeds, fencing was necessary, and barbed wire was the best solution to their problem.

As the ranchers planted new grasses and fenced their property, the price of beef skidded. Excellent grazing conditions in the summer of 1887 encouraged some of the smaller ranchers to continue their open-range policy, but the corporations were reeling. The Swan Company of Wyoming folded; the Niobrara Cattle Company of Nebraska followed the Swan into receivership. Creditors pressed them, and beef prices fell, from $2.40 a hundred pounds in spring, 1887, to $1.90 by the next fall. Prices continued low for the next half dozen years as Texans continued to sell the longhorns at the low price and farmers unloaded their small herds as a drought returned the unfavorable grazing conditions.

Ranching clearly was changing. The long trail drives had virtually ceased. Roundups occurred less regularly because of the fences. Cultivated grass was an especially important commodity. And farmers arrived in growing numbers. Many observers felt the great disaster of 1886-87 and the ensuing changes marked the end of the cowboy era. Charlie Russell wrote to his friend George W. Farr about "tracks in history that the farmer can't plow under," and sketched a complicated but symbolic picture of the demise of the West, showing the cowboy and his friends yielding to Dame Progress. Frederic Remington expressed the end of the era even more dramatically with his

Cattle in blizzard on plains, 1886. **Harper's** scene could be anywhere; this was the desperate winter that devastated the herds throughout West.

painting entitled **The Fall of the Cowboy.** Showing a wizened puncher opening the gate of a barbed-wire fence, Remington included two elements that brought down the cowboys: the fence and the snow. "What has become of them?" novelist Owen Wister asked in **Harper's Magazine.** "Three things swept him away—the exhausting of the virgin pastures, the coming of the wire fence, and Mr. Armour of Chicago, who set the price [of beef] to suit himself. But all this may be summed up in the word Progress."

An era ended. That is undeniable. But perhaps the changes took more of an emotional toll than technical. "It was a great task to reorganize the machinery of ranch work," and "cut down the cattle outfits," Clay wrote, but he and his counterparts on the other spreads had it done within a year. The acreage in hay increased dramatically from around 56,000 in 1880 to more than 300,000 in 1890 in Montana alone. Mowing machines, hay rakes, and ditch-digging tools became important parts of the cowboy's regalia, commented one observer. "Cowboys don't have as soft a time as they did. I remember when we sat around the fire the winter through and didn't do a lick of work for five or six months of the year, except to chop a little wood to build a fire to keep warm by. Now we go on the general roundup, then the calf roundup, then comes haying—something that the old-time cowboy never dreamed of—then the beef roundup and the fall calf roundup and gathering bulls and weak cows, and after all this, a winter of feeding hay. I tell you times have changed. You didn't hear the sound of a mowing machine in this country ten years ago."

It was with mixed emotions that the editor of the Denver **Field and Farm** newspaper urged change upon his readers. "There is progress even among the cowboys and stock-growers on the plains," he wrote in 1886. "We have before noticed the fact that the use of guns in some cases is prohibited. The rough, hurrah style of handling cattle, we are told, has become unpopular. . . . If this thing goes on long this way, the ideal cowboy will soon disappear, and we shall have to content ourselves with a knowledge of him through reading the history of the 'Wild West.' In fact, the typical vaquero is fast disappearing and a new class of bovine gentlemen are taking the place of

Preceding pages: Looking
for strays. Below: Urging herd
toward branding corral.

the former. Cattle raising is becoming a more legitimate business than it has been."

Ranchers also began to make better use of their land. Most turned to irrigation as a way of increasing the hay output, but some even irrigated just for the benefit of the stock. Much to the distaste of the old ranchers, several members of their fraternity even turned to sheep raising, but it was an economically sound decision, because sheep could forage in grass already given up on by cattle.

With the arrival of more settlers, ranching in Montana and Wyoming rapidly became limited to privately owned pastures and irrigated forage. The Johnson County war is only the best-known outbreak of hostilities between settlers and cattlemen. There were other less violent conflicts, but they soon dwindled to common animosity, for both law and inertia were on the side of the farmers. Open-range cattle raising was no longer a financially profitable endeavor except in the best of conditions, conditions which the settler often did not affect.

Another sign of the well-being of ranchers was the numerous stock-raisers' associations that sprang up simultaneously. Indicative of both the prosperity and hardship, they were organized after ranching proliferated and the cowmen developed similar problems. The associations supervised roundups and recorded members' brands, but also attempted to keep intruders out of ranges that were feeding all the cattle they could support, fought rustlers and prairie fires, and offered bounties for wolves. They usually began as local associations, then burgeoned to regional chapters, and finally territory-wide groups that went so far as to set up their own courts to settle disputes between members. By 1885 these associations blanketed the West, demonstrating both the cattleman's penchant for self-government and their fear of intruders.

The associations' high-handed acts, such as the Johnson County war, and the death of thousands of cattle in the 1886-87 winter because of bad planning and neglect turned a large segment of public opinion against them. From then on, cattlemen had to fence their lands to limit the number of stock on a particular range, and they had to be sure that they had not overgrazed, for they could not afford another such disaster. Nor would the public that bought the beef stand for it.

Ranchers apparently were suffering in part from a bad public image. Before ranching came to the Great Plains, it had been historically a temporary use of the land that preceded settlers and farmers. When they arrived, making more intensive use of the land, ranching moved on to other unsettled lands. When they discovered the Great Plains, however, cattlemen thought they had an area that would never be of use to farmers, and that the range cattle industry could perpetually exist there. Much as the proponents of slavery claimed that it had reached the "natural limits" of the tillable soil. But they continued and found that the ranchers were wrong. Irrigation proved how fertile the "American Desert" could be. A group of southwestern cattlemen finally complained to the President: "Though bitterly attacked by the hostile part of the press and some members of Congress, the nature of our pursuit and the character of the men engaged in it have prevented us from responding to defamations and calumnies that seem to have well-nigh convinced the public mind that the man who has, or has had, an interest in cattle on the range is little better than a highwayman, and a bandit worthy of penal reprobation." The ranchers hoped that improved methods of ranching, better business techniques, and better public relations would help their image.

With the improvement of ranching techniques, settlers moved more rapidly into range land, forcing cattlemen to run their beeves only on their own land, encircled by barbed wire. Southern cattle still arrived on the northern range, but by rail instead of trail. The days of the gigantic spread were gone. More human-sized ranches became the rule, although some of them remained as large as 750,000 acres.

As barbed wire spread, need for a general roundup ceased. The end of the traditional western cattle industry is described in the official wording of the Wyoming Minute Book of the Board of Live Stock Commissioners. On April 4, 1905, "a call was made and published giving notice of the stockmen of a meeting to be held in the office of the Commission . . . to arrange the roundups and appoint commissioners therefor. As no stockmen appeared, the annual circular was not ordered. There being no further business, the meeting adjourned."

8

"a prehistoric race"

Legends surrounding the cowboy make it extremely difficult to focus on any reality that might be hidden in the recesses of history. A descendant of the romantic vaquero of Mexico and the hardworking "cow boy" tradition of the deep South, the American cowboy is heir to a rich heritage. Some insist that the heritage is Biblical; English historian Arnold Toynbee theorized that America was returning to the pastoral ways of Judea of old when it was interrupted by the Industrial Revolution. Joseph McCoy, who opened Abilene, Kansas, to the Texas longhorns a century ago, noted with pride that "all men must acknowledge that the vocation of live stock is not only ancient, but of old, as now, altogether honorable in the highest degree."

Although the cowboys themselves insisted on the occupation's honor, they were more interested in its adventure and believed that they were taking part in a historic drama. Why else would hundreds of them have stood before an old five-by-seven-inch view camera, dressed in their Sunday best, with looks befitting a Napoleon or a Caesar? The unusual number of first-person narratives written by cowboys who, in many cases, were not even born until the twentieth century also testify to their inordinate desire to record their experiences for history. Will Tom Carpenter, a cowboy who wound up managing a ranch in the Big Bend of Texas, thought of the "life" he knew in terms of "the wild & wooly west, among wild women, wild men, and everything else that might be called wild." J. F. Tripplett, who confessed that his "notes . . . may never do me any good," also succumbed to self-contemplation: "All except myself are asleep; I am sitting near the camp fire, writing notes . . . I am too much of a night owl to go to bed early. . . . If Mr. Indian gets my scalp he'll be sure to make gun wads or a bonfire of this book."

This same sense of making history led others to document the cowboy in pictures. The famous Montana painter Charles M. Russell felt he had arrived in the West just as the cowboy had reached his peak. His paintings accurately preserve the flavor and authenticity of the range and its men that Russell loved. "You woldent know the town or the country eather," Russell wrote his friend Bob Stuart in 1913 (with his highly individual style of spelling in full flower). "Its all grass side down now. Wher once you rod Circle and I night rangled a gopher couldent graze now. The boosters say its a better country than it ever was but it looks like hell to me. I liked it better when it belonged to God." Frederic Remington, an easterner trained in art at Yale, was captured by the same desire to document a way of life that he felt was quickly passing, and his paintings and sculptures have interpreted the cowboy to generations of Americans. Probably the best document of the cowboy, however, is the photography of Erwin E. Smith, a young man from Bonham, Texas, "who played cowboy all the time." "To know and retain for others the intimate things as to detail of cowboy life," said Smith in later years, "is the real reason why I have made such an inexhaustible study of life on the range with a camera."

The life that Remington, Russell, and Smith set out to record attracted many young men. Russell himself was one of them, for he left home at age sixteen to share the romance of the West. Russell's parents permitted him to go, hoping that he would get "the West" out of his system and return home to manage the family business, but they, like so many others, waited in vain.

President Theodore Roosevelt also cited adventure and the opportunity to prove oneself as part of the attraction of the cowboy life. Roosevelt often relaxed on his Dakota Bad Lands ranch and enjoyed touring the West while he was in office. Following a 1905 speech in Fort Worth, he joined cattlemen Samuel Burk Burnett and W. T. Waggoner on a wolf hunt in Indian Territory. Under the guidance of John Abernathy, the famous wolf hunter, the party succeeded in killing several wolves, Abernathy catching them from horseback with his hands, a feat that tremendously impressed the enthusiastic Roosevelt.

"Isn't that wolf biting you?" Roosevelt asked Abernathy when he realized the hunter's hand was in the animal's mouth. Abernathy pointed out that his hand was behind the wolf's teeth and could not be bitten.

"Oh, I see," responded the President, "but how do you get your hand behind those teeth?"

"By practice, Mr. President," replied the truthful Abernathy.

Pleased by the entire affair, Roosevelt wrote his son Kermit that "I want to have the whole party up at Washington next winter." He later appointed Abernathy a U.S. marshal.

The adventurous life also appealed to farm boys. Although he grew up following a plow, James Emmit McCauley watched cowboys ride and patterned his actions after theirs. "My first wishes and desires was to be a wild and woolly cowboy," he recalled when he set down his reminiscences. "The more I saw of them drifting west, the more determined I was to be a cowboy." His opportunity came when, tired of hazing by his classmates, he stabbed the school bully in the ribs with his common everyday Barlow knife and left home before the authorities arrived. But his flight was more that of newly gained freedom than the desperate lunge of a criminal. He ran home, kissed his mother good-by, and, as he recorded in his memoirs, "turned my face to the setting sun."

The teenage McCauley was not unusual, for most cowboys were young, the average age twenty-four. They usually entered the job expecting to stay with it the rest of their lives, but few reached retirement age on the back of a horse because the job required youthful enthusiasm and strength. Short-lived careers are shown in statistics from the Spur Ranch in Texas, although wandering cowboys also account for the numbers. During the two decades after 1885, 901 cowboys worked on the Spur, three percent for as many as five seasons, but sixty-four percent for only one. Some simply gave it up and took another job. Foreigners often returned home to regale their friends with stories of adventure and fun in the American West. And others stayed on the ranch, where they became wranglers or cooks, jobs not quite so demanding as rounding up, branding, or trail driving.

Cowboys came from many different beginnings—black,

Bar Diamond Bar cowboy reclining on his horse probably was clowning for photographer Smith, TX, 1905-10.

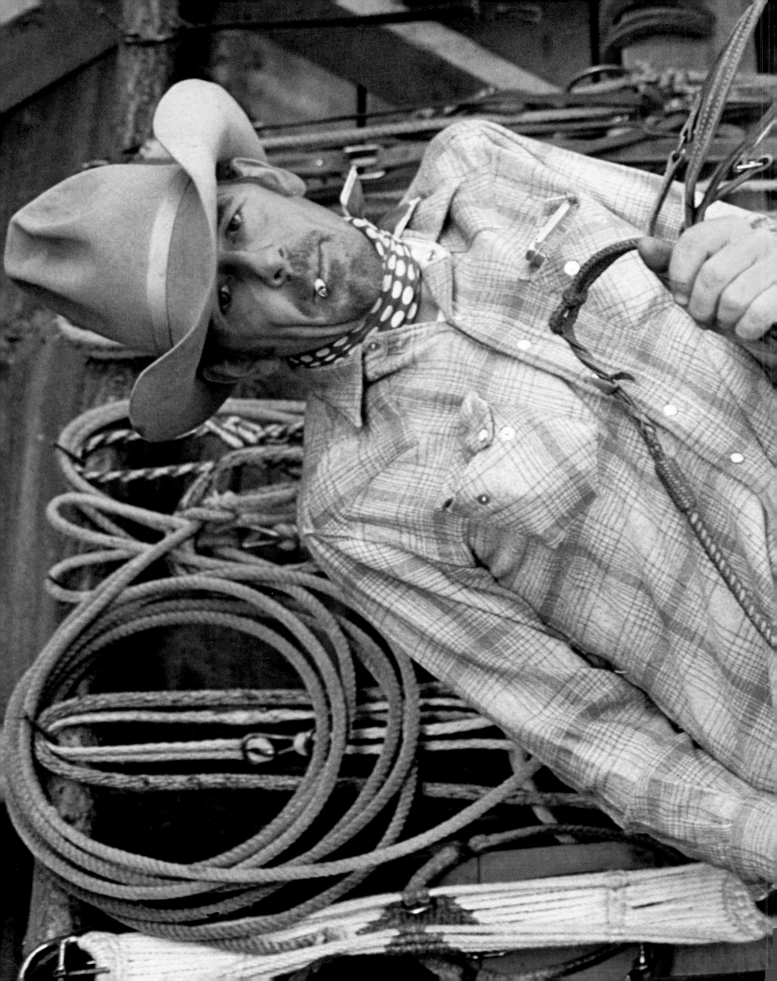

brown, and white. The first of them were native Mexicans and Southerners who grew up around cattle and earned their living from them. After the Civil War, many men who knew only how to ride turned to working cattle because of the countless opportunities. A decade later, cowboys came from still different sources. By the 1880s, any combination was possible. Of fifty-three cattlemen interviewed in Wyoming in 1885, forty were American-born and thirteen were from foreign countries. Sixteen states were represented in the total, as were England, Ireland, Canada, Scotland, Germany, France, and Russia.

Philip Aston Rollins, a collector of western Americana who visited many cowboys in the West during the last two decades of the century, was particularly interested in "England's delegation." Although there were members of the middle class in the West, he noted that most of the Englishmen were the "delightfully companionable, mildly reprobate, and socially outcast members of the gentry and nobility." They never identified themselves as such, of course, but took pseudonyms that were betrayed by such small slips as mentioning the result of an English university boat race. "Thank God, we won!" said one displaced scholar, revealing his birthright. Rollins concluded that the "West contained more than one signet ring, cut with ancestral arms and studiously hidden under a flannel shirt." The international mix is still evident on the range today, whether in the Ivy League graduate looking for adventure, the "tenderfoot" from the city vacationing on a relative's ranch, or the son of an Australian or South African rancher in the United States for an education in the ways of the American cowboy.

Most of the cowboys were American-born, usually of English, Irish, or Scotch descent. But a large number were Mexicans and Negroes, Mexicans having inherited the trade from their fathers, the blacks being taught it while in servitude in Texas. There were even a few Indian cowboys, trained originally, perhaps, by the brown-robed Franciscans who tended the missions in Spanish Texas.

Some ranchers and cowboys were in the West because of poor health, leading a New Mexico cowman to comment that it seemed that every easterner with consumption and a few thousand dollars entered ranching. The "champagne air" did revive many on the verge of collapse; Colonel O. W. Wheeler of California and President Theodore Roosevelt among the better-known convalescents. Others were in the West to pursue the gentlemanly life, which until the hard winter of 1886-87 and the ensuing collapse of the cattle industry, was relatively easy to find in places like the Cheyenne Club of Wyoming or the Montana Club, in Helena.

Some cowboys worked simply for work. Jobs came easy because the ranches usually were short-handed, and the work was seasonal, so there was a large turnover. Kentuckian J. F. Tripplett found himself on an 1862 roundup in the Humboldt and Truckee river country of Nevada. "Here I am on my way into the heart of a country known to be inhabited by hostile Indians; all for the paltry sum of ten dollars a day," he noted in his journal.* "And why? Because I have the misfortune to be broke."

Cowboying also attracted fugitives from justice. A lonely life, it gave one the opportunity to go for days without seeing a person outside

*—An extraordinarily high figure for the man and for the time. Perhaps he meant ten dollars a week.

Cowboy with rifle—posed or shooting
a snake. Turkey Tracks Ranch,
TX, 1910.

the normal group. It made a good refuge, because cowboys were accepted as
honorable persons until they proved otherwise. Fugitive James McCauley
remembered that he was never troubled by the law as long as he was on the
range. Only when he returned home did the sheriff try to arrest him. Several
infamous figures spent a few weeks or months herding cattle northward to the
railhead. Sam Bass spent the time prior to his great train robbery herding
cattle up the trail, and Billy the Kid rode well enough to steal horses from
John Chisum, who had employed him.

The common denominator of all the cowboys was the
combination of skills that are becoming increasingly rare: the ability to break
wild horses, the instinct necessary for a roundup, a knack for the hard work of
branding. But within the requirements of work, the cowboy's imagination can
soar. He can be the knight of the prairies or the hardworking handyman. That
is his freedom.

As inalterably associated with the cowboy as hard work is
his character, which inevitably impressed visitors to the camp. One characteristic that seemed to Rollins remarkably consistent was courage, without
which one could not ride a horse. Working cattle exposed men to dangers not
encountered in the normal surrey ride. If a man "lost his nerve" riding, he
could no longer cowboy. Physical injury was almost guaranteed.

Cheerfulness seemed to be the antidote to the hard, dirty
work a cowboy did. Combined with the normal reserve the westerner had for
strangers, cheerfulness produced a pleasant bearing. Both were based on
rarely seeing anyone. Because the newcomer might be a horse thief, he had to
be regarded with suspicion. But because he might simply be someone on a
long trip who needed help, he had to be offered a minimum of hospitality. The
cowboy did not take too much interest in his visitor's gear or ask questions
about his past. But when the newcomer had established himself, such hesita-
tion diminished, the visitor was made more welcome, and curiosity often
found an outlet in casual conversation.

That the cowboy looked up to and respected women is
well known. Teddy Blue Abbott penned the often-quoted phrase about a cowboy fearing only two things: "a decent woman and being set afoot." There is
abundant evidence that he was right. Cowboys liked femininity and always set
their women on pedestals. One of Rollins' friends summed it up this way: "If I
ever have to get married, I'm going to marry a woman what's all over gol-
durned fluffs." Another rebuked a woman in the presence of other cowboys
when she made a forward remark: "For God's sake, woman, why can't you let
us look up to you?"

It was the opinion of Agnes Morley Cleaveland that the
frontiersmen were more chivalrous than others. Running a ranch in New
Mexico toward the end of the nineteenth century, Mrs. Cleaveland recounted
numerous instances in which chivalry was practiced. She was accustomed to
cowboys offering her deference, even to the point of purposely losing at parlor
games. But a most unusual—and to her symbolic—incident occurred one
night as she rode back alone from the mail box to the ranch. She encountered
another rider, who courteously moved his horse off the road so she could

pass. When she arrived safely at the ranch, she learned that he was a robber with his saddlebags full of gold and the only thing that stood between him and freedom in Mexico was a fresh horse. He had allowed Mrs. Cleaveland to pass unharmed, although she had a good saddle horse, and had been killed by the sheriff while trying to steal a new mount a few miles down the road. Not only were westerners more chivalrous, concluded Mrs. Cleaveland, but "gun fights between men, or even horsestealing, carried with them something of sportsmanship, which . . . at least removed them from the realm of rank cowardice," where she placed many of the "sex horrors of today [1941]."

Cowboys can be so short-spoken that their language takes on native descriptiveness—"vivid and down to earth," as the folklorist John A. Lomax observed after years of talking with and studying cowboys. Cowboys themselves were aware of word usage, saying of a sentence: "Bobtail her and fill her with meat." A talkative visitor in camp was often advised to "save your breath for breathing." The cowboy speech was epigrammatic. He often invented words, or used known words as other parts of speech. An undesirable character "sifted" into camp. Of the Grand Canyon it was said: "God dug that there hole in anger, and painted it in joy."

Many other words might be used to describe the cowboy character, but perhaps the most common—and ironic—is independent. True, the cowboy enjoyed a certain kind of independence, but a kind that made him happy because he was doing what he wanted rather than one that allowed him freedom within his job: roundups, trail driving, roping, branding, riding, fencing (or "building pastures"). He was not free to turn down a task assigned by the foreman, although he would not perform the same tedious chore too often. Many cowboys swore that they would have quit their job if they had been asked, for example, to build fifteen miles of fence rather than simply repair one.

An incident that seemingly contradicts the traditional image of the loner cowboy-type occurred near Tascosa, Texas, in 1883. Twenty-four cowhands on three large ranches struck for higher pay. They also demanded an increase in wages for their foreman and the cook. Their number quickly grew to 200, but they were fighting overwhelming odds, including tough ranchers unwilling to succumb to pressure and drifters willing to work for less than the strikers were demanding. The strike was soon called off and the chastened punchers returned to work, the incident to serve as an exception to the code of loyalty to the ranch and the independent, anticooperative myth of the cowboy. The following year the Knights of Labor organized the cowboys on a number of West Texas ranches into local assemblies and endured until 1887, when the Knights collapsed nationwide.

Often the independence enjoyed by the rancher is confused with that of his hired hand, the cowboy. While the cowboy was perennially in need of money and forced by necessity and spirit to work from horseback, the rancher became a businessman capable of making or changing the course of western affairs. But he, too, gave up much of his personal independence when he joined in stockmen's associations in an effort to preserve the open range, lobby in Congress, and combat rustlers. The image that remains

Top row (l to r): Three Bell
Ranch cowboys, Padlock cowboy.
Bottom: Padlock wagon cook,
Bell cowboy, Padlock veteran,
Bell cowboy with Foreman
Don Hoffman (dismounted).

today blends the cowboy with the rancher, taking the better part of both to produce a myth that existed only in separate people in separate parts of the country at different times.

Part of the popular image of the cowboy is his dress, now fashionable world-wide. The boots, hat, chaps, the colorful silk scarf and stylized spurs, are standout fashion accessories as well as historical symbols. While most of the western accoutrements are only decorative today, they all originated, like many fashion classics, from practical designs and functions. Many items, such as the hat, had regional variations, but a few superlative designs were universal.

The usually soft, smooth felt hat, contrary to the Hollywood image, was often black, although more usually dove-gray or light brown. Today the most popular color among cowboys is "silver belly"; the still-brisk demand for black hats is perhaps an effort to combat the popular "good guys" commercialism that some cowboys have come to resent. The old-fashioned hat had a cylindrical crown about seven inches high and usually cost the cowboy two to six months' salary. The brim was always wide against sun and rain. A belt, sometimes highly ornamental and occasionally of silver or gold woven wire, silver conchas, or rattlesnake skin, hugged the crown. Most of the cowboy hats were made by Stetson and Company, which only recently ceased production. Sometimes a Mexican sombrero substituted for the more popular "Texas" or "Montana" style hat if the puncher lived in the Southwest.

Hats are even in vogue among urban residents who seldom if ever visit the range. Manufacturers in Fort Worth and San Angelo, Texas, and Sheridan, Wyoming, for example, produce their own hats and styles, like the "Whistle Special," made by "Whistle" Ryon of Fort Worth and embodying one of the hundreds of unique creases for a hat. Bull riders, cutting-horse riders, and many others have their own special crease, worn like a badge and called different names in different parts of the country. Today hats are made of rabbit fur, beaver fur, and several other kinds of fur. The brims are not quite so wide as the nineteenth-century hats, running from three and one-half to four inches, probably because it is easier to tuck the smaller hat into the cab of a pickup. The hat is usually about six and one-half inches high before creasing. Although often mass-produced and less expensive today, the hat still fulfills the function it did years ago, and a working cowboy will pay from $30 to $125 for his headgear.

One of the cowboy innovations that has spread to women's fashion is the handkerchief-cum-bandana. Worn mainly as a mask, it was usually made of cotton—the only material at the general store. The stereotyped red bandana was an alternative to readily available white, but the cowboy would get silk if he could. The handkerchief usually hung loosely around the neck, so it could be quickly slipped up over the face in dust. The bandana often is used today to keep the back of the neck from becoming sunburned under a short-brim hat.

The cowboy's shirt was usually wool or cotton, collarless and starchless. It was often checked or striped, but never red, a color punchers believed upset the cattle. The cowboy's taste was somewhat conserva-

210

tive, influenced by his limited choice at the general store, although he usually wore garters on his shirt sleeves in recognition of the custom of the day. His basic plainness showed in undistinctive coats and trousers. They were usually wool, somber in color, black or brown leather at their most impressive. Suspenders would have bothered him and a tightly buckled belt was likely to cause injury on a bucking horse. So the cowboy often wore no belt, unless he came from the Southwest, where he might have picked up a Mexican red or green silk sash for a touch of Latin flair.

The vest is still a popular garment among cowboys working in hot climates. It replaces a coat, allowing more freedom and ventilation. It is mainly a source of additional pockets rather than a piece of clothing, a less crushable location for tobacco. When dressed up, the cowboy wore a woolen waistcoat especially made for the western trade. His overcoat was light brown canvas, blanket lined, with skirts down to the knee. The exterior was sometimes painted—yellow—to make it windproof. Even now the synthetic overcoats, or slickers, made for the cowboy trade are yellow, in the tradition of the rowdy Charles Russell paintings.

The cowboy wore gloves in winter and while roping. Some men wore gloves all year long, an expression of vanity, according to Rollins, who claimed that the gloves showed the cowboy was so good at roping that he did not have to do the more menial tasks. Gloves were probably made of horsehide or buckskin, in a distinguishing yellow, gray, or greenish cream-white color, with a flaring gauntlet of about five inches. In the northern ranges the stylish gloves were traded for practical mittens of knitted wool.

Some cowboys wore tight-fitting brown or black leather cuffs for further protection. Stiff and extending four or five inches from the wrist, the cuffs were adjusted by buckled straps. These provided protection for a sensitive part of the arm against painful rope burns.

The cowboy's footwear was also important. His black, high-topped, high-heeled boots soon became the object of much attention and styling. In the beginning they were simply utilitarian, and although it is often claimed that the heels were high to keep the rider from putting his foot all the way through the stirrup and being dragged by his horse, Will S. James, the cowboy preacher, could think of no more compelling reason for high heels than the "same motive that prompts the girls to wear the opera heel." The vamps, the part of the boots that cover the instep and toe, are made of thin, pliable leather of the best quality. The legs are usually the same or of top-grade kid. Tops were level, but as style became more important the front was occasionally made higher than the back, and the side of the boot was decorated with fancy stitching. The tall legs shielded the cowboy's legs against rain, adding leather protection where his chaps left off. In cold weather he wore an additional pair of heavy socks and overshoes. Many old-time cowboys complain of cramped toes, leaving a false image of poorly constructed footwear, but the cramped toes are another mark of vanity rather than bad boots, since the cowboy always insisted on a tight fit.

The cowboy admitted that spurs were worn for both business and social reasons. The heavy metal with blunt rowels was intended as

Spur cowhand of seventy years ago sits his horse like contemporary on following page.

much for hanging onto a bucking horse as for "spurring" a horse to greater speed. In fact, many spurs had a "buck hook" that the cowboy could snag on the saddle cinch to help him stay on a frisky horse. Rowels were usually about one-half inch long, but Mexican spurs, copied in the Southwest, had rowels as long as two and one-half inches. A leather strap across the top of the boot combined with two chains under the instep held the spur in place. Of course, there were many different kinds of spurs, some even worn "upside down" (depending on your point of view, section of the country, and favorite style). In addition to the conchas or intricacies sewn or cut into the leather, the spurs make a decorative noise when the cowboy walks. "Danglers" often were added to amplify the sound.

Chaps were not so frivolous as their shape, protecting the riding cowboy, as they did, from brush, cacti, rain, and cold weather. Their dramatic appearance was enhanced by their texture, for they were made of heavy, dehaired leather, or the shaggy skin of a bear, wolf, dog, goat, or sheep. They were most often white, although style again dictated color for many cowboys. He wore chaps when riding, but also in town or in the presence of a woman. Along with his vest, gun, and spurs, the chaps constituted his "Sunday-go-to-meeting" uniform.

Sometimes the cowboys dressed outlandishly. When Chinch, a Negro cowboy on the Noonan Ranch near Castroville, Texas, was going to get married, Frank Collinson, fresh from England and without a cow pony, traded him two suits of English clothes, a trunkful of starched shirts, and a handful of neckties for his horse. Collinson did not comment on how the formally dressed Chinch was received in town. Teddy Blue Abbott set the style on the Montana range. After finishing a trail drive, Teddy went to North Platte, Nebraska, bought some new clothes, and had his picture made. "I had a new white Stetson hat that I paid ten dollars for and new pants that cost twelve dollars, and a good shirt and fancy boots. They had colored tops, red and blue, with a half-moon and star on them," recalled Abbott. "Lord, I was proud of these clothes! They were the kind of clothes top hands wore, and I thought I was dressed right for the first time in my life." His sister earned his disdain, however, when she judged that he looked "like an outlaw." "I told her to go to hell," said Abbott. "My sister was a fool anyhow."

In the northern range, cowboys were supplied a fur coat and cap by the rancher for winter use. Cowboys usually were responsible for their own clothing and gear, but a fur coat of buffalo skin or wolf pelt was so expensive that cowboys could hardly afford them. Thus the rancher "encouraged" the cowpuncher to go out into the teeth of a Montana blizzard to break the ice in the drinking pond for the cattle.

The cowboy also had several popular, unnecessary accessories. One was horsehair chains, which were used in courting because all women were supposed to adore them. The horsehair chain was laboriously and sometimes excellently woven from horsehairs plucked from the rider's favorite steed. Highly decorative, it made a flashy watch chain, if the cowboy was fortunate enough to have a watch. Today horsehair chains can be found in local history museums commemorating the pioneers of the cattle industry,

Carl Darr, an old Four
Sixes puncher, has become
a noted saddle maker
for cowboys. This is his
shop in Paducah, TX.

Padlock cowboys breaking
camp disassemble a
range tepee. Bedrolls
are in foreground.

and are still marveled at by those who understand the patience required for a man of action like the cowboy to plat such an obviously tedious rope.

Although most romanticists identify the cowboy with his hat, the cowboy would more likely have fought for his saddle. There were literally dozens of different kinds of saddles, for in some instances, like Mexico, the cowboy made his own. The basic saddles, however, are the stock saddle (or cow saddle or range saddle) and the English saddle (or the kidney pad, human saddle, or postage stamp, as the cowboys called it).

The basic design of all saddles is similar. For the cow saddle, the cantle is high enough to prevent a roper from slipping backward after his horse squats on its haunches when he ropes the cow. If the roper was a Texan and tied his lariat to the horn of the saddle, the horn would also be high. The width and length of the seat depends on the rider's choice, as does the slope toward cantle or horn and the inclination of the horn.

The saddle is designed according to the form of the tree, or frame; California, Brazos, White River, Nelson, Oregon, Cheyenne are some of the styles. For a roper the saddle must be of strong construction to stand strain. The front of the tree was bolted to a metal horn, then everything covered with rawhide and fastened to a broad, curved leather plate, called the skirt, which rests on the horse's back. The jockey is laid over the top of the skirt and fitted around the base of the horn and cantle. A roper's saddle might have a roll, a long welt protruding for about a third of an inch on the face of the cantle to keep the rider from sliding backward when roping.

There are several methods by which the saddle can be cinched to the horse: Spanish (rim fire), center rig, three-quarter rig, or double-cinch rig. The owner of the saddle chooses. The terms Spanish (or rim fire), center, and three-quarter simply refer to the point at which the cinch is attached to the saddle, with the Spanish rig meaning that the cinch is attached near the front of the saddle and that it will be under the front of the horse's belly. The three-quarter rig gives a roper better balance in that the cinch is a bit further back on the horse's belly. The center-fire rig is the commonest single-cinch rigging, meaning that the cinch is under the center of the horse's belly. The double-rig cinch is for heavy roping. Originating in Texas, it provides a front and rear cinch, the most reliable arrangement of all.

If the undersurface of the saddle is smooth, which is usually the case, a saddle blanket is used. Two strands of stirrup leather hang from the saddle in unequal lengths, with the longer end being looped through the stirrup and tied to the shorter end. No buckles were used, because the cowboy wanted a saddle he could repair on the range if something broke. The stirrup itself is made of a bent piece of wood, bolted together at the top and strong enough to protect the cowboy's foot if the horse should fall on it. If the cowboy wants to be a bit fancier he can add a wedge-shaped piece of leather called the **tapadero** in Spanish, or in the shortened form, **tap.** The term translates as cover or hood.

Two sets of leather thongs hang from the saddle, one set in the front and the other in the back, and can be used for tying whatever might be laid over the horse behind the cantle—usually a slicker or bedroll.

219

The front set might hold a frying pan, food, or some piece of equipment. The cowboy might also have a buck strap on the horn of his saddle. Top riders scorn it, but those who favor safety want some extra help should the horse start bucking.

Of course, there are many options for the saddle. Sometimes the rider might have a pair of leather pockets called "cantinesses" or saddlebags behind the cantle. In desert country he might want water canteens. The saddle weighed thirty to forty pounds with all its gear.

The saddle was the most expensive piece of equipment for the puncher, costing up to ten months' wages depending on the elaborateness of the design. The leather usually was carved or covered with stitching or ornaments. Sometimes the cowboy added his own decoration, made of brass nails or perhaps glued-on rattlesnake skins. Cheaper saddles are usually cherry-red in color, but most range saddles are brown.

A good saddle was highly valued. It gradually began to fit the form of the rider and became more comfortable for him. Thus he would not want to lose his saddle, or even loan it out. Many stories tell of cowboys who gambled away everything but their saddle, and the expression, "He's sold his saddle," means that a cowboy is financially or morally insolvent.

The western saddle was an all-around good piece of

equipment. Roping was possible; riding the bucking horse was possible; long rides on slightly wild horses were possible. The "night herd," requiring the cowboy to stay in the saddle all night and keep watch on the cattle, was possible because the saddle was so large that he could sleep in it. Also, the saddle made a good pillow for ground sleep.

The cowboy had other pieces of equipment essential to his work. Perhaps the best known among the children playing "cowboys and Indians" is the rope, lariat (a contraction of the Spanish term **la reata**), or lasso (from the Spanish **lazo,** meaning a snare or slip knot). Rope was the commonest term; reata was used in Wyoming. In the early range days the rope was made of buffalo skin. In later days rawhide or Texas hemp was used. Ropes usually were about one-half inch thick if they were made of rawhide, three-quarters inch in diameter if made of hemp. Four to eight strands were braided together until the rope reached forty to seventy feet in length. A loop was made by passing one end of the rope through the hondo, or honda, usually a strong piece of rawhide or metal in the form of a "U." Texans used the longer rope because of their habit of dallying—tying one end to the saddle horn. The term comes from another corruption of a Spanish term, **dar la vuelta,** meaning to give the rope a turn around the horn. It soon became "dale vuelta," "vuelted," and finally "dallied," the term known all over the cow range.

Also on the saddle hung the quirt, a foot-long, flexible, woven piece of leather. The upper end was loaded with lead heavy enough that the cowboy could hit a rearing horse to prevent him from falling backward and killing the rider. Two thongs were attached to the lower end, and a loop on the upper end could be slipped over the cowboy's wrist so he would not drop the quirt. It was used to whip the horse when the cowboy wanted a faster gait.

Other implements among the cowboy's collection were a horsehair line used to picket the horses, a hobble rope (sometimes two leather cuffs connected by a chain, sometimes a piece of buckskin), and a bridle. The western cowboy used a bridle similar to those used around the world. Old-time cowboys insist that you can tell a great deal about the ability of a horseman by looking at his bridle and bit, and that famous cowboys, like Charles Russell, the cowboy artist, were not good horsemen because they used bridles and bits that gave them the most control over the horse.

A common bridle consisted of a single strap, slit at the top so it could be pulled over the horse's ears, with the two ends connected by an adjustable buckle. Sometimes a finely plaited leather or horsehair bridle was used instead of the straps. The bridle could be made as elaborate as the cowboy wanted. One man even had a bridle of woven silver wire. The reins connected to the bridle could be tied at the saddle end or not. Most riders left them untied, thinking that there was less chance they would become entangled in them if they should be thrown from the horse.

Many cowboys insisted that the horse did not have to be tied to a hitching post, because he had learned through experience not to question appearances. Fastened to the reins was the bit, a thing of beauty to the maker and owner, but almost always a torture tool for the horse. There are several kinds of bits, giving the rider various degrees of control over the horse. Perhaps the most painful to the horse is the spade bit, which has a piece of metal shaped like a putty knife three or four inches long that presses down on the horse's tongue when the rider pulls the reins. The spade bit was probably the most common on the range. The ring bit does not have the "spade," but adds the feature of a ring that encircles the horse's lower jaw, pressing against a sensitive nerve when the rider pulls the reins. The bit has a rounded piece of metal called a port in place of the spade. The ring is connected to the port. The half-breed is a gentler bit, with neither a spade nor a ring, but only a port, which looks like a narrow croquet wicket, that is about two and one-half inches high, with a bar (and sometimes a roller on the bar) across it. The curb bit is the simplest and most humane, but gives less control over the horse. The port is lower; no roller is used. Finally, an experienced rider might use a hackamore, which is nothing but a leather strap instead of a bit. The hackamore can shut off the horse's wind, but cannot otherwise hurt him.

Some cowboys added various other items to their bit to give them better control over the horse. Intended to suggest pain rather than cause it, the bit might be rigged with a piece of barbed wire or other metal. Such additions were not popular, however, because the cowboy liked to control his horse by skill rather than torture.

Cowboys still ride the western range and think and carry themselves similarly to their cousins of a hundred years ago. The American cowboy is a world-wide hero, and the word itself is recognized in almost every language. Yet the cowboy has changed. "Your kind were never plenty but thair Scarce these days," Charles Russell wrote to his friend Bob Thoroughman in 1920. "These were the kind of men that brought the spotted cattel to the west before the hump backed cows were gon. Most of these people live now only in the pages of history, but they were regular men Bob and you were one of them." Teddy Blue put it more succinctly. "It's not like that now," he wrote as he closed his memoirs. "We were a prehistoric race."

9

a living myth

Cowboys today combine the historic and the contemporary, the myth and the reality. Engaged—as herders—in one of man's oldest professions, they employ helicopters and Cessnas to rout contrary steers out of brushy patches. They are history in a contemporary setting, real characters amid booted and string-tied fakes. They have been dragged feet first into realization that today's United States is a hostile place for iconoclastic idealists who shun the present-day business world.

The historic cowboy, in fact, avoided the business end of the operation. He prodded his steers up the trail to market, then depended upon his naive honesty to attract a fair bid for his cattle. Currently cowmen must face the perpetual producer-squeeze—ever-spiraling expenses on the one hand and decreasing sales on the other. Whereas the nineteenth-century cowman often had the opportunity to choose among several independent buyers, today's seller faces only a few large combines with power to influence the price simply by staying out of the market. And this buyer-seller confrontation is rendered considerably more complicated by consumer pressures. Frustrated cattlemen recently responded to decreasing prices, increasing feed costs, and rather naive criticism by staging several "cattle executions," which attracted nation wide publicity but did little to solve the rancher's dilemma.

Amid such news it is easy to believe that the old-fashioned cowboy no longer exists. A **Puck** magazine writer declared as early as 1913 that, "The West is no longer wild. . . . Where the stage-driver used to crack his whip over the backs of his eight horses, the Rural Free now creeps along, bearing catalogues of dress-goods and seventeen-dollar suits for men. It used to be called 'The Trail.' It is now a Star Route. . . . It may be an effeminate age; but the solemn truth must be told: the rough stuff no longer gets over. The only typical cow punchers left in the country, who still cling to the picturesque costume of other days, are a few fakers selling Mexican diamonds and some side-show barkers at Coney Island. The other cow-punchers wear mercerized underwear, red ties, and work a union or eight hour day."

The West that survives has changed. Fencing brought improved breeds, new grasses, scientific techniques. Men like the Klebergs of the King Ranch have tackled the foremost problems facing modern ranchers. Pragmatic goals have directed their thoughts. In the 1890s, Richard Kleberg tried to induce rain by explosive concussion, and drilled some seven hundred feet deep for water with newly developed bits. Several decades later his grandson, Robert Jr., took on the problems of underdeveloped nations, an ironic goal considering the aloofness usually associated with the ranch that became known as "the Walled Kingdom." Declaring that he wanted to put the men, techniques, and purebred animals of the King Ranch where they were most needed, he set out to change barren deserts into pasture, to teach Cubans, Venezuelans, and Moroccans how to handle cattle Texas-style, and, ultimately, to provide food for the starving masses of the world. His legacy is the world-wide King Ranch with its more than 350,000 head of cattle. His King Ranch-developed grasses have turned barren land into pasture, and the Santa

Preceding pages: Bell Ranch wagon boss takes a chew of Red Man.

Gertrudis cattle endure much better in tropical and subtropical climates than other breeds.

Despite the image that persists in cigarette commercials, cowboying also has changed. When the mule-drawn chuck wagon and bed wagon became uneconomical, the Klebergs remodeled pickup trucks and loaded the chuck box and cooking equipment onto the bed. Some large ranches have followed suit, claiming that the "motorized" chuck wagon covers greater distances and keeps up better with the cowboys. The 06 Ranch at Alpine, Texas, and the ZX Ranch in Oregon are two of the other big outfits that have adopted the motorized wagon. The old, freshly painted chuck wagon usually is in the barn, held for the visit of a photographer or the annual Frontier Days parade.

Some ranchers have not yet given up the mule-drawn wagon, insisting that it is more economical. Benny Binion, of Jordan, Montana, and Las Vegas, Nevada (where he is owner of the Horseshoe Casino), admitted that he liked the mule-drawn wagon better because he likes to do things in the old ways, but also claimed that it saved him money. "The way I look at it is that there are two things that can't be modernized," he said. "Picking fresh fruit and handling livestock. If you were out here in the middle of this ranch at night and then had to go plum' back to the house to sleep, it would be ten o'clock before you got there. With a wagon, men can sleep right here by their job and get up bright and early the next morning right where they work. And if it comes a rain, you are stuck with a pickup, but with these wagons, you just go on." Other cowboys point out that the cattle work better early in the morning before the flies get to them and before it gets too hot. The wagon enables them to get to the cattle quicker.

Contrary to the simple, nature-oriented cowboy are the large number of machines creeping onto ranches in the name of efficiency. A Pikes Peak rancher has cowhands who do not even use ropes. If the cow needs attention, they herd her back to the barn and treat her there, where they have the proper instruments. In California at least one rancher's son has taken up the motorcycle, and one Canadian cowman herds his cattle with a snowmobile during the blizzard months. More common are helicopters used on ranches like the Waggoner in Texas and the Tequesquite in New Mexico.

Although they will never get rich quick, cowboys earn more money today than ever before. Salaries range from $275 a month plus room and board for an inexperienced hand to $800 a month for a top wagon boss. Most start out at around $400 per month with room and board, and receive a quick $25 per month raise if they turn out to be good hands. When they are hired as extra hands for the roundup, cowboys are sometimes paid by the day instead of the month—$16 per day plus chuck and a place to put down their sleeping bag. At least one cook, a professional who owns his own motorized wagon and hires out to various roundups, gets $35 per day. Cowgirls are hired on several ranches as part of a husband-and-wife team, but relatively few women work cattle.

Today's cowboys are as versatile as their nineteenth-century counterparts, because they have to cook, chop wood, fix fence, herd

cattle, rope, brand, and perform other maintenance tasks. On some ranches this includes fixing the machinery when it breaks down. The foreman of the Binion Ranch admitted that he would not hesitate to ask a puncher to do any legitimate job, although he dared not request that they spend too much time, say, fixing fence. "They'd take their bedroll and head down the road if I did that." The buckaroos of the ZX Ranch in Oregon are more specialized. "They are so independent," the buckaroo boss said, "they don't even want to feed their own horses."

Even rustling has changed to become more efficient. In the past a thief had to be a good cowboy himself to herd the cattle off the owner's range without being caught. He had to round them up, drive them off, then find a quiet place where he could spend several days changing the brands. He also had to be quite an artist with a "running iron," because most ranchers had designed their brands specifically so that they would be hard to alter. Today a rustler might spot the herd he wants from the air, enter the ranch with a trailer-truck, put some bait in front of the trailer, and simply wait for the cattle to walk onto the truckbed. He does not have to change the brand, because the beeves are usually sold and slaughtered within hours of the theft.

The dramatic changes that have come to ranching in the last fifty years have created mild paranoia in some old-time cowmen. Just as the long drive from Texas to Kansas was the "badge" that many nineteenth-century drovers wore with pride, so the contemporary cowboy relishes the aura of the trail. There are still some trail drives on the larger ranches that might last as long as a week, but more often cowboys now must take to the highway to complete a drive of any length at all. Thus Frontier Days celebrations usually find a dozen or so cowboys bringing a chuck wagon and a few head of cattle into town just in time for the opening rodeo. Benny Binion recalled how he missed his last chance for a real drive when a railroad strike paralyzed transportation between Sierra Blanca, in West Texas, and Fort Worth in 1920. The ranchers had gathered up their wagons and cattle, and were about to leave for Fort Worth when the strike was settled. "I was never so sick," recalled Binion. "Didn't get to make that trail."

Binion only missed a trail drive; some cattlemen have virtually given up the horse. They drive pickup trucks out to look over their cattle or to visit the roundup camp. They swoop down in helicopters to herd cattle out of brush or box canyons, jobs formerly reserved for the fast rider. These same cattlemen do not feel that they have contradicted the code of the rancher, because they have only moved in a direction that expediency seemed to dictate. Grappling with the stick of his helicopter, one New Mexico cowman could think of no more appropriate metaphor than, "Dammit, this is just like riding a bucking horse."

But the strain that created cowboys in the nineteenth century still lives. The nature of cowboying—not the work—has changed because of the configuration of most modern ranches. Texas, New Mexico, Colorado, California, Washington, and Arizona ranches are cross-fenced to the point that a man could not ride out across country with his bedroll without encountering a depressingly large number of fences. Only in Montana, Wyoming, Nevada, Idaho, and Oregon are there still millions of acres unfenced. The largest pasture on the 6666 Ranch at Guthrie, Texas, is about 17,000 acres, quite small compared to acreage that used to comprise a 6666 pasture. Smaller enclosures mean that roundups do not take as much time, and that cowboys do not have to spend weeks and months camping out with the roundup crew. They can lead more "civilized" lives, spending nights in the bunkhouse or with their families, leading several old-timers to insist that real cowboying is a lost art. People like Bill Bailey are not so sure. A native Texan who moved to California to manage a ranch, he got into cowboying because "my father was a cowpuncher, and his father was a cowpuncher—and I just kinda kept it going. I'll never say stop 'cause he never did." A thoughtful man who relishes his privacy, Bailey observes that if "cowboying is obsolete" it is "a great life gone."

One of the only places in the country where a cowboy can get the feeling that time has not passed him by is the Matador Cattle Company in Nevada. Few large spreads in Nevada are fenced, but the Matador comprises between one and two million acres, much of it Bureau of Land Management land, with few fences, even along the highways. The Matador is still a roundup outfit, where the cowboy must commit himself to six uninterrupted months on the range, eating off the chuck wagon, and sleeping on the ground.

Most of the big ranches keep ten or twelve cowboys on full time year round. At roundup time they often hire extra men, sometimes as many as ten or fifteen. There are few good cowboys looking for work, according to the manager of the 06 Ranch. Binion's ranch foreman confirms the

229

Line camp in Big
Horns has no electricity
or running water.

situation. "You have to hire almost anybody who comes along and claims to be a cowboy," he reported. Part of the reason there are few good hands looking for jobs might be the working conditions. A cowboy has to love what he does, because he still must work from daylight to dark, seven days every week on most of the large ranches. "I never give 'em a vacation," claimed Binion. "I never give 'em nothing. They got to figure a way to get it. They got to figure out how to get anything from me. I don't give 'em nothing but a good job." Benny Binion does not even give his hands time off to go to Sunday morning church. "I would never hire a man who did not believe in God," he claimed, "and I would never hire a man who goes to church." Many beginners are able to get jobs by boasting of experience, because ranchers do not often check references. "You might like him and I might not," said Benny, "so I don't ask you what you think of a cowboy." But it doesn't take a good foreman long to spot a faker. A casual toss of the loop, a stab at roping a calf is sufficient to separate the pros from the aspirants.

To provide better cowhands, several Wyoming ranchers joined resources in 1966 to form a school for cowboys in the Centennial Valley. Young men from all over the West learned how to saw off a calf's horns, how to brand and doctor a calf, and the two ways to castrate a sheep—with a knife and with a cowboy's teeth. Thirty-nine students ranging in age from fourteen to twenty-five gathered at the old V-Bar Ranch near Laramie to listen to animal nutritionist Robert Hatch lecture on cattle anatomy, to learn how to sit a bucking bronco, and to learn the basics of irrigation, fertilization, livestock feeding, machinery repair, and artificial insemination. The Mountain States Ranch School was the brainchild of a local businessman who wanted a school that would be of more use in the West than a Job Corps Center. Although supported by funds from rancher Lyndon Johnson's War on Poverty, the school probably turned out few dyed-in-the-wool cowboys, because even the instructors admitted that students hoping to buy a horse saved their money in vain, because horses were of little use on a modern ranch.

Ranching was an industry of closely related, clannish cattle barons in the nineteenth century, and despite their independent character, still remains so today. In fact, the clan grows smaller as large ranches are chopped up to avoid inheritance taxes, and the sons and grandsons take over the remaining spreads. Increasingly, the contemporary ranch manager is likely to be college-educated, with a background in business management, animal husbandry, and administration. He seldom loses money. According to one Fort Worth rancher, only the people interested in ranching as an investment are losing money. The real ranchers are hanging on, he said, and the bad years and the good years tend to average out, giving a respectable profit. Without pausing to consider the question, Binion declared that he had never lost money on his ranch. "Haven't made much in some years," he admitted, "but never lost a dime."

Some would-be cowboys have adopted the ways of the range, thinking that the lore of Wild Bill Hickok, Billy the Kid, or Bat Masterson is the legitimate heritage of the frontier. They relish the imagined excite-

233

Tack room, horses
facing outward from
rope corral, horse
being shod. Most cowboys
are responsible for
shoeing own string of
six to twelve mounts.

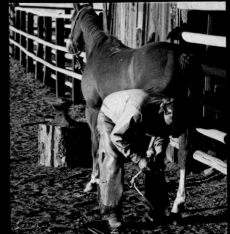

Wagon haircut, on the range.

ment of bunkhouse free-for-alls, the grudge-precipitated-by-a-challenge fight, and the brawls and shootout orgies in the cattle towns. But sufficient information exists to show that that West never was. The "quick-draw" gun duel never occurred. The fact that a man can draw and fire a pistol in less than half a second is more proof that the "classic" confrontation never happened than proof that it did. There are, of course, abundant stories of the classic gun duel, but all seem to have a fatal flaw. The overriding principle is that a man who knew that it is possible to draw and fire a gun so fast would never allow his opponent to draw first. Wild Bill Hickok did gun down gambler Phil Coe in 1871, but the most reliable account of the incident insists that both began firing, gun in hand, or that Bill drew and shot Coe after Coe had turned his back. Probably the nearest episode to the classic gunfight occurred in Quanah, Texas, in 1893. Texas Ranger Captain Bill McDonald and Childress County Sheriff John P. Matthews met in the street between the opera house and the train station. They talked, then drew their guns and started firing. McDonald fell wounded, Matthews dead. But even the circumstances of this encounter cannot be proved, for the newspaper reported that "it was impossible to tell who fired the first shot," the duelists or a member of the crowd. In fact, the fatal shot might have come from "another source."

So any puncher who chose one of these legendary heroes to follow would be hard put to find historical data to match the dime novel and television exploits that probably attracted him in the first place. Nor did the gunfighters hold themselves up as examples of anything except self-survival. **Gunsmoke's** Matt Dillon might give his enemies a chance to draw first, but Wild Bill did not. He lasted as long as he did (only to be shot in the back) by placing survival above any other consideration.

The gun, in fact, was not part of the cowboy's legitimate heritage. Paintings by Remington and Russell show the puncher with a pistol, even while seated around the campfire at dinner, but the documentary photographs of Erwin Smith and L. A. Huffman seldom reveal a six-gun on any of their subjects. That some nineteenth-century cowboys packed guns is amply shown by the numerous diaries that record the almost ceremonial strapping on of the pistols as they left Doan's Crossing headed into Indian Territory, where they might justifiably need a gun. When asked why he wore a pistol, Bud Powers replied that you might never know when you're going to need it, an attitude reflected by a contemporary Montana puncher who keeps his pistol in his bedroll. But the fact remains that most cowboys shunned the weapon as bulky, heavy, and cumbersome. It got in the way.

Despite all the changes on a modern ranch, real cowboys trained in the ways of working cattle and loving the open range have survived. Numbering probably fewer than 800, they are the hard core who treasure their independence, travel from ranch to ranch each year, and live and talk cattle and horses. They consciously strive to set themselves apart from the grind of industrialism and mechanization. And they share a terrific esprit de corps. Their relationship with the ranchers is illustrated in the story told by Benny Binion. As he was leaving his ranch at the end of a summer season, he met a cowboy coming in the back door. "Are you here to visit or stay, Wade?" Binion

236

asked. "To stay," Wade replied. "Well, I'll see you this fall, then," Binion said, meaning that Wade was hired on and that he would be spending the ensuing months on the range. As simple as that.

To help his fellow punchers find real, old-time outfits to work for, J. M. Brooks of Hardin, Montana, a cowboy with a few head of wild horses, published a small pamphlet called **Horse and Cattle Ranch Job Opportunities and Information,** which, in the tradition of the West, he illustrated himself. He tells fellow cowboys which ranches still run the team-drawn chuck wagon and bed wagon, which ranches will let a cowboy do real cowboy work rather than tie him down to simple ranch chores. Also included are such mundane but useful facts as how much they pay and who to contact, but the listings are limited to those outfits that a real cowboy would work for. The book has received little publicity, but the hand-to-hand circulation among cowboys makes it one of the most thumbed pamphlets on the range, for cowboys are always interested in seeing another part of the country.

The endurance of esprit de corps is more dramatically seen in the case of a buckaroo who became terminally ill. The ranch first sent him to the Mayo Clinic, then offered to send him and his family on a trip anywhere in the world. But he turned them down, saying, "Can you imagine me wanting to do anything other than what I'm doing right now? This is all I want to do—just be here with these guys, ride out every morning. How could anyone be happier?"

The real cowboys left know each other. They meet on the various ranches and talk about cowmen, foremen, cattle, and horses. They are men who work the cattle in the old ways and forego the luxury of the bunkhouse each night. They are members of one of the smallest fraternities extant, and consider themselves absolutely independent of any other influences—besides their horse, the cow, and the great outdoors. These men

Three styles of living:
Don and Charlotte Hill (l)
with daughter at
summer line camp, where
Ms. Hill cooked for
buckaroos; Jack Cooper (r)
with daughter in living
room of Padlock camp
house; ZX bunkhouse. Below:
Contrary to movies,
cowboys do not kiss horses.

are the direct descendants of the independent-minded cowboy of a century ago, who jumped from job to job when he got bored and prided himself on quick rope work and sure control of a semiwild mustang.

Slick roping and riding have earned thousands of dollars for some cowboys. Beginning in 1885 and 1886 county fairs across the West featured "cowboy contests" with prizes ranging up to $50 for "the best time in catching, saddling, and riding a wild bronco." Shows sprang up throughout the West, but the Denver show was perhaps the largest, for it attracted 12,000 enthusiastic viewers in 1886. The events appeared so brutal to the secretary of the local humane society that he wrote a letter to the editor of the local paper threatening to arrest the entire Chamber of Commerce if the punishment did not stop. The newspaper approached the story somewhat tongue-in-cheek, but apparently the Chamber of Commerce feared action. Three of the day's six events were cancelled as the rodeo continued into the second day. "The audience expected to see the Humane Society step in and stop the show," reported the newspaper. "But the H.S. had its eye on the steer. It did not see the cowboy."

Just a few months later in faraway London, Queen Victoria watched in amazement as Buffalo Bill presented his troupe of rough riders in a command performance during her Golden Jubilee celebration. It was quite an honor for Bill, who had started his touring Wild West Show just four years before. Hoping to present the real story of the West to the world, he had brought together some of the best riders, ropers, shooters, and all-round good showmen the West had to offer, and had taken them on a tour of the United States. The show started with good horsemanship, but quickly proceeded to an illustrated history of the West, complete with Indian fights, stagecoach robberies (the Deadwood stage, of course), and even a reenactment of Custer's Last Stand. His 1887 show in London marked the Queen's first public appearance since the death of her consort, Prince Albert, so Bill found himself in the midst of quite a celebration. On one occasion he had King Leopold II of Belgium, King Christian IX of Denmark, King George I of Greece, King Albert of Saxony, and the Prince of Wales riding in his Deadwood stage. "Colonel, you never held four kings like these before," said the Prince of Wales, a poker player.

"I've held four kings," said Cody, "but four kings and the Prince of Wales makes a royal flush such as no man ever held before."

Buffalo Bill's "cowboy fun" was "the greatest, most unapproachable, thoroughly howling success that America ever sent to London," concluded Marshall P. Wilder, the American dwarf comedian and writer.

Buffalo Bill's touring show, coupled with the success of events like Denver's rodeo, led cities across the West to stage similar events. Soon real talent emerged from the cowboy's ranks. In Oklahoma the 101 Ranch realized how much ability it hoarded when the ranch's cowboys presented a rodeo for visiting journalists. Bill Pickett, a genuine "sweat and dirt" cowboy on the 101, rode his speckled horse Spradly up alongside a rampaging bull, jumped off on the animal's neck, slid around to the front to get a hold on the bull's lip with his teeth, and then let go! The bull went down every time.

243

The only time the bull didn't go down was when Bill and the 101 were in Mexico City. The local bullfighters challenged him to try that trick with a Mexican fighting bull. Believing in his cowboy, Zack Miller, the ranch owner, bet against the locals and made the event the feature of his afternoon program. Bill held onto the hellbent cuss for fifteen minutes, but he could not get a grip on the animal's lip, and the bull would not fall. Colonel Zack and Bill barely managed to escape with their lives, as the locals insisted that the pot was theirs, while Miller insisted that by hanging on for the allotted time Pickett had won. The **Rurales** saved them that time.

Another 101 alumnus was gum-chewing, rope-twirling, twangy-voiced Will Rogers, who was so bashful that his entire act at first consisted of spinning a lariat. But he found that his eyes and mouth were not busy during the twirling, so he started talking to the audience, and they loved it. Soon the rope-twirling became secondary, as the Cherokee Indian from Oklahoma shared his homespun philosophy with his audience. "Everything is funny as long as it is happening to somebody else," he offered. Or: "Politics has got so expensive that it takes lots of money to even get beat with."

The Wild West show and rodeo were unqualified successes. Gradually they added events until the full-blown presentation that eager fans see in Fort Worth, Houston, Denver, Calgary, Cheyenne, Pendleton, etc. was intact. As successful as rodeo is, it inspires divergent opinions among working cowboys. Some feel that it is the proper receptacle for their skills, which have been made obsolete by changes on the range. "The old ways are going—on all the ranches—and good riddance," snarled a hardbitten old Texan who has lived through most of the changes. "That's the place for roping," said a Colorado rancher of the rodeo, "and all the other old ways." On the other hand, rodeo cowboys are often ridiculed by working cowboys, perhaps out of envy, but ostensibly out of disdain for their lack of real skill. They might be able to rope, ride, and bulldog in the arena, but can they do it time and time again on the range, then drag the calf over to be branded or whatever, all day long? Most cowboys realize that rodeoing is only for the strong, brave, and talented, but also believe that it does not require the same stamina that day-in-day-out work on the ranch does.

Another argument that still rages around rodeo is treatment of the animals. Members of the humane societies decry the continual riding of horses, forcing them to buck by means of a buck strap until the horses are literally too old to perform. Even worse, they say, is bull-riding, for it is much more awkward for a bull to buck and pitch than for a horse. No one says the animals are treated any more roughly in a rodeo than they are on the range. The objection has been that the treatment is inflicted in the name of sport. While the cowboy does not have much sympathy for such opinions, he does agree that the continual roping of a calf might be a bit mean. The Rodeo Cowboy Association has now insisted that all calves used in calf-roping and bulldogging be a minimum weight. It is, of course, an argument that will hardly be settled immediately.

That the modern cowboy is beneficiary of a rich heritage cannot be questioned. But more than a few of today's punchers are confused

as to what that heritage is. Those who come by their inheritance honestly can recall a father and grandfather who punched cattle and broke horses. They can recall the manliness, the solitude, the quiet strength, the brief but pungent conversations. They recall the honesty with which their forebears dealt with their neighbors. They recall the intelligence with which they went about their daily tasks.

The modern cowboy still has quite a reputation even in the international field. During World War II, while the United States and Great Britain were locked in combat with the Nazi terror, Cambridge University chose not a historian or a social scientist, but Professor of English J. Frank Dobie of the University of Texas and formerly of the cattle range in Uvalde County to "explain Britain's chief ally." In 1952, when the motion picture **High Noon** first appeared, showing a brave, honorable sheriff who knew he had to meet a ruffian gang in a showdown, but who still allowed the gang all the rights and honor due a normal citizen before the confrontation, it was studied abroad for clues to American foreign policy.

But the modern cowboy remains in the American West, intellectually and physically isolated, and self-sufficient. "I don't really feel that I have any special relation with people ranching up here 100 years ago," commented Benny Binion. "I don't really. I'm a modern-day rancher, and I make a living and keep up my health by ranching. I never lost a year on this ranch. I can stay right here and make money, even now at the price beef's bringing."

epilogue

The cowboy today, although less numerous than he was a century ago, is still very much in evidence, as Bank Langmore's pictures throughout this book make abundantly clear.

Cowboying itself has become somewhat more mechanized. Some modern punchers use squeeze chutes for doctoring cattle, rather than roping them on the open range. They may chase the herds on a motorbike, snowmobile, or helicopter, or ride to their morning's work in a pickup truck with horses in a trailer behind. Yet in their essentials the immemorial tasks of the cowboy are remarkably unchanged. Comparison of Langmore's pictures with the now-historic photographs of Erwin E. Smith appearing on the text pages, and even with the nineteenth-century illustrations from **Leslie's** and **Harper's Weekly,** reveals more similarities than differences in the men, the animals, and the land. No one pictured in this book would have any difficulty recognizing anyone else.

Cowboy clothing and equipment have always been ingeniously functional; it would be surprising if any of it had changed, except for the technological improvements conferred by contemporary materials. Yet even here significant alterations are few. If medium-lay nylon rope is easier to come by than braided leather reatas, there is still no substitute for leather saddles, chaps, and boots, felt hats, or cotton Levis. No one has yet come up with a good plastic spur.

Scientific breeding has undoubtedly improved the taste and texture of beef, and in the process eliminated the spectacular but too-long longhorns. But white-faced Herefords are an almost equally ancient race. They suffered the blizzard of 1886 on the Great Plains, and their descendants, with perhaps slightly more marbling in the lean, are still among us.

Likewise the mustang. He is no longer the wild horse of the prairies, but even with more controlled breeding he is quick, smart, and enduring, and no one has taught him different or better ways for trailing, cutting, or otherwise herding cattle.

The grazing land of the West still looks much as it did, although the grasses are better and the formerly endless spaces are now finite. The acreage of large contemporary ranches is now counted in the hundred thousands rather than the millions.

Thus, despite changes, an association, an interdependence, persists. Partly this is so through circumstance. Partly it is because Americans would not have it any other way.

Two conditions assure the cowboy's survival. One is the myth that has created almost unexcelled pride in the cowboy species. Nineteenth-century America hailed the man who conquered the Great Plains, saluted him as the new breed necessary for the winning of the West. This admiration did not stop with the demise of the trail drive and the first wave of fiction, but has continued—and been embellished—by western artists, by photographers, in serious literature and the movies. Altogether they have made the cowboy a hero.

The cowboy's survival is also assured by the men themselves. The vaqueros along the Mexican border, the buckaroos of Oregon and Nevada (and contiguous areas), and the cowboys of the other western states continue in the tradition and pride of their predecessors. The King Ranch vaqueros take pride in their cattle and horses, even in the special grass developed to feed them. Wyoming punchers believe that the best ropers in the West sit at their campfires. And the buckaroos of Oregon feel second to none.

Such exhilaration makes it easy to forget that cowboying is essentially hard physical labor, though not unmixed with fun. For all the sweat, roping, branding, steer wrestling, and bronc riding are also sport. Cowboys enjoy their work and have pride in their skills. The roundup is still a sort of neighborhood celebration. On the O6 Ranch at Alpine, Texas, marachi musicians serenade the gathering as cowboys put finishing touches to the fall roundup, the final event in the cycle of beginning and ending that is so necessary for human renewal.

And while today's cowboy knows that the number of huge ranches is dwindling, and that increasingly he is a member of an elite group, he continues to perpetuate the established tradition. He asks only that it be allowed to continue, that his children may enjoy the same feeling of accomplishment while doing what they would rather do than anything else in the world: be a cowboy.

Cowboy and mount overlooking Canadian River, in Texas Panhandle, 1908.

bibliography

Books

Abbott, E. C., and Smith, Helena Huntington. **We Pointed Them North: Recollections of a Cowpuncher.** Norman: University of Oklahoma Press, 1955.

Adams, Andy. **The Log of a Cowboy.** Lincoln: University of Nebraska Press, 1968.

Adams, Ramon F. **Come an' Get It: The Story of the Old Cowboy Cook.** Norman: University of Oklahoma Press, 1952.

_____. **The Cowman & His Philosophy.** Austin: The Encino Press, 1967.

_____. **The Horse Wrangler & His Remuda.** Austin: The Encino Press, 1971.

_____. **The Old-Time Cowhand.** New York: The Macmillan Company, 1961.

_____. **Western Words: A Dictionary of the Range, Cow Camp and Trail.** Norman: University of Oklahoma Press, 1944.

Alter, Judith MacBain. "The Western Myth in American Literature and Painting of the Late Nineteenth and Early Twentieth Centuries." Unpublished Ph.D. Dissertation, Texas Christian University, Fort Worth, 1970.

Atherton, Lewis. **The Cattle Kings.** Bloomington: Indiana University Press, 1961.

Bard, Floyd C., as told to Agnes Wright Spring. **Horse Wrangler: Sixty Years in the Saddle in Wyoming and Montana.** Norman: University of Oklahoma Press, 1960.

Billington, Ray Allen. **Westward Expansion: A History of the American Frontier.** 2nd Ed. New York: The Macmillan Company, 1960.

Blasingame, Ike. **Dakota Cowboy: My Life in the Old Days.** New York: G. P. Putnam's Sons, 1958.

Bolton, Herbert Eugene. **Texas in the Middle Eighteenth Century: Studies in Spanish Colonial History and Administration.** Austin: University of Texas Press, 1970.

Boorstin, Daniel J. **The Americans: The Democratic Experience.** New York: Random House, 1973.

Branch, Douglas. **The Cowboy and His Interpreters.** New York and London: D. Appleton and Company, 1926.

Carpenter, Will Tom. **Lucky 7: A Cowman's Autobiography.** Austin: University of Texas Press, 1957.

Clapham, Walter C. **The Movie Treasure: Western Movies: The Story of the West on Screen.** London: Octopus Books Limited, 1974.

Clay, John. **My Life on the Range.** Chicago: Privately Printed, 1924.

Cleaveland, Agnes Morley. **No Life for a Lady.** Boston: Houghton Mifflin Company, 1941.

Collings, Ellsworth, and England, Alma Miller. **The 101 Ranch.** Norman: University of Oklahoma Press, 1937.

Collinson, Frank. **Life in the Saddle.** Ed. and arr. by Mary Whatley Clarke. Norman: University of Oklahoma Press, 1963.

Connor, Seymour V. **A Biggers Chronicle.** Lubbock: Texas Technological College, 1961.

Cook, James H. **Fifty Years on the Old Frontier as Cowboy, Hunter, Guide, Scout and Ranchman.** Norman: University of Oklahoma Press, 1954.

Dale, Edward Everett. **Cow Country.** Norman: University of Oklahoma Press, new edition, 1965.

_____. **The Range Cattle Industry: Ranching on the Great Plains from 1865 to 1925.** Norman: University of Oklahoma Press, 1960.

Dobie, J. Frank. **Cow People.** Boston, Toronto: Little, Brown and Company, 1964.

_____. **The Longhorns.** New York: Grosset & Dunlap, 1941.

_____. **The Mustangs.** Boston: Little, Brown and Company, 1952.

Duke, Cordia Sloan, and Frantz, Joe B. **6,000 Miles of Fence: Life on the XIT Ranch of Texas.** Austin: University of Texas Press, 1961.

Durham, Philip, and Jones, Everett L. **The Negro Cowboys.** New York: Dodd, Mead & Company, 1965.

Dyskra, Robert R. **The Cattle Towns.** New York: Alfred A. Knopf, 1968.

Fletcher, Baylis John. **Up the Trail in '79.** Ed. with Intro. by Wayne Gard. Norman: University of Oklahoma Press, 1968.

Frantz, Joe B., and Choate, Julian Ernest, Jr. **The American Cowboy: The Myth and the Reality.** Norman: University of Oklahoma Press, 1955.

French, William. **Some Recollections of a Western Ranchman, New Mexico, 1883-1889.** New York: Argosy-Antiquarian Ltd., 1965. 2 vols.

Forbis, William H. **The Cowboys.** New York: Time-Life Books, 1973.

Ford, John Salmon. **Rip Ford's Texas.** Ed. by Stephen B. Oates. Austin: University of Texas Press, 1963.

Gard, Wayne. **The Chisholm Trail.** Norman: University of Oklahoma Press, 1954.

Garrett, Julia Kathryn. **Fort Worth: A Frontier Triumph.** Austin: The Encino Press, 1972.

Haley, J. Evetts. **Charles Goodnight: Cowman and Plainsman.** Norman: University of Oklahoma Press, 1936.

_____. **George W. Littlefield, Texan.** Norman: University of Oklahoma Press, 1943.

_____. **The XIT Ranch of Texas and the Early Days of the Llano Estacado.** Norman: University of Oklahoma Press, 1953.

Hassrick, Peter. **Frederic Remington.** Fort Worth: Amon Carter Museum of Western Art, 1973.

_____. **Frederic Remington: Paintings, Drawings, and Sculpture in the Amon Carter Museum and the Sid W. Richardson Foundation Collections.** New York: Harry N. Abrams, 1973.

Hassrick, Royal B. **Cowboys: The Real Story of Cowboys and Cattlemen.** London: Octopus Books Limited, 1974.

Hastings, Frank S. **A Ranchman's Recollections: An Autobiography.** Chicago: The Breeder's Gazette, 1921.

Hine, Robert V. **The American West: An Interpretive History.** Boston: Little, Brown and Company, 1973.

Holden, William Curry. **Alkali Trails, or Social and Economic Movements of the Texas Frontier, 1846-1900.** Dallas: The Southwest Press, 1930.

_____. **The Espuela Land and Cattle Company: A Study of a Foreign-Owned Ranch in Texas.** Austin: Texas State Historical Association, 1970.

Hollon, W. Eugene. **The Great American Desert.** New York: Oxford University Press, 1966.

_____. **The Southwest: Old and New.** New York: Alfred A. Knopf, 1961.

Horgan, Paul. **Great River: The Rio Grande in North American History.** New York: Holt, Rinehart & Winston, 1954. 2 vols.

Howard, Robert West, and Arnold, Oren. **Rodeo: Last Frontier of the Old West.** New York: Signet Books, 1961.

Hunter, J. Marvin. Ed. **The Trail Drivers of Texas.** Nashville: Cokesbury Press, 1925.

Hutchinson, W. H. **California: Two Centuries of Men, Land, & Growth in the Golden State.** Palo Alto: The American West Publishing Company, 1969.

James, Will S. **27 Years a Mavrick, or, Life on a Texas Range.** New Ed. Austin: Steck-Vaughn Company, 1968.

Jones, Mat Ennis. **Fiddlefooted.** Denver: Sage Books, 1966.

Kennedy, Michael S. Ed. **Cowboys and Cattlemen: A Roundup from Montana: The Magazine of Western History.** New York: Hastings House, Publishers, 1964.

Kennon, Bob, as told to Ramon F. Adams. **From the Pecos to the Powder: A Cowboy's Autobiography.** Norman: University of Oklahoma Press, 1965.

Knight, Oliver. **Fort Worth: Outpost on the Trinity.** Norman: University of Oklahoma Press, 1953.

Lea, Tom. **The King Ranch.** Boston: Little, Brown and Company, 1957. 2 vols.

Lewis, Willie Newbury. **Tapadero: The Making of a Cowboy.** Austin: University of Texas Press, 1972.

McCauley, James Emmit. **A Stove-Up Cowboy's Story.** Intro. by John A. Lomax. Dallas: Southern Methodist University Press, 1943.

McCracken, Harold. **The American Cowboy.** Garden City, New York: Doubleday & Company, 1973.

McDonald, Archie P. Ed. **Hurrah for Texas: The Diary of Adolphus Sterne, 1838-1851.** Waco: The Texian Press, 1969.

McDowell, Bart. **The American Cowboy in Life and Legend.** Washington: National Geographic Society, 1972.

McLean, Malcolm D. **Fine Texas Horses: Their Pedigrees and Performance, 1830-1845.** Fort Worth: Texas Christian University Press, 1966.

Madison, Virginia. **The Big Bend Country of Texas.** Rev. Ed. New York: October House, Inc., 1968.

Matthews, Sallie Reynolds. **Interwoven: A Pioneer Chronicle.** Austin: University of Texas Press, new edition, no date.

Meigs, John. **The Cowboy in American Prints.** Chicago: The Swallow Press, Inc., 1972.

Meinig, D. W. **Imperial Texas: An Interpretive Essay in Cultural Geography.** Austin: University of Texas Press, 1969.

Murphy, Lawrence R. **Philmont: A History of New Mexico's Cimarron Country.**

Albuquerque: University of New Mexico Press, 1972.

Myres, Sandra L. **The Ranch in Spanish Texas, 1691-1800.** El Paso: Texas Western Press, 1969.

Nordyke, Lewis. **Cattle Empire: The Fabulous Story of the 3,000,000 Acre XIT.** New York: William Morrow and Company, 1949.

——————. **Roundup: The Story of Texas and Southwestern Cowmen.** New York: William Morrow & Company, 1955.

Osgood, Ernest Staples. **The Day of the Cattleman.** Chicago: University of Chicago Press, new edition, 1957.

Renner, Frederic G. **Charles M. Russell: Paintings, Drawings, and Sculpture in the Amon G. Carter Collection.** Austin: University of Texas Press, 1966.

——————. **Paper Talk: Illustrated Letters of Charles M. Russell.** Fort Worth, Texas: Amon Carter Museum of Western Art, 1962.

Ridge, Martin, and Billington, Ray Allen. Eds. **America's Frontier Story: A Documentary History of Westward Expansion.** New York: Holt, Rinehart, and Winston, 1969.

Rogers, Will, and Russell, Nancy C. **Good Medicine: The Illustrated Letters of Charles M. Russell.** Garden City, New York: Doubleday, Doran & Company, Inc., 1930.

Rollins, Philip Ashton. **The Cowboy: His Characteristics, His Equipment, and His Part in the Development of the West.** New York: Charles Scribner's Sons, 1924.

Russell, Don. **The Wild West, or, a History of the Wild West Shows.** Fort Worth: Amon Carter Museum of Western Art, 1970.

Savage, William W., Jr. Cowboy Life: **Reconstructing an American Myth.** Norman: University of Oklahoma Press, 1975.

Siringo, Charles A. **A Texas Cowboy, or Fifteen Years on the Hurricane Deck of a Spanish Pony.** Intro. by J. Frank Dobie. New York: William Sloane Associates, 1950.

Skaggs, Jimmy M. **The Cattle-Trailing Industry: Between Supply and Demand, 1866-1890.** Lawrence: University of Kansas Press, 1973.

Stephens, A. Ray. **The Taft Ranch: A Texas Principality.** Austin: University of Texas Press, 1964.

Sullivan, Dulcie. **The LS Brand: The Story of a Texas Panhandle Ranch.** Austin: University of Texas Press, 1968.

Surface, Bill. **Roundup at the Double Diamond: The American Cowboy Today.** Boston: Houghton Mifflin Company, 1974.

Timmons, William. **Twilight on the Range: Recollections of a Latterday Cowboy.** Austin: University of Texas Press, 1962.

Tinkle, Lon, and Maxwell, Allen. Eds. **The Cowboy Reader.** New York, London, and Toronto: Longmans, Green and Company, 1959.

Vanderbilt, Cornelius, Jr. **Ranches and Ranch Life in America.** New York: Crown Publishers, Inc., 1968.

Van Zandt, K. M. **Force Without Fanfare: The Autobiography of K. M. Van Zandt.** Ed. by Sandra L. Myres. Fort Worth: Texas Christian University Press, 1968.

Wallis, George A. **Cattle Kings of the Staked Plains.** Denver: Sage Books, rev. ed., 1964.

Ward, Fay E. **The Cowboy at Work: All About His Job and How He Does It.** New York: Hastings House, Publishers, 1958.

Webb, Walter Prescott. **The Great Plains.** New York: Grosset & Dunlap, 1931.

Westermeier, Clifford P. Ed. **Trailing the Cowboy: His Life and Lore as Told by Frontier Journalists.** Caldwell, Idaho: The Caxton Printers, Ltd., 1955.

Articles

"Across the Continent," **Leslie's Illustrated,** December 29, 1877.

"Among the Cow Boys," **Harper's Weekly,** October 2, 1880.

"Among the Cow-Boys," **Harper's Weekly,** November 27, 1880.

Bell, James G. "A Log of the Texas-California Cattle Trail, 1854," ed. by J. Evetts Haley, **Southwestern Historical Quarterly,** XXXV (January and April, 1932), XXXVI (July, 1932).

Bishko, Charles Julian. "The Peninsular Background of Latin American Cattle Ranching," **Hispanic American Historical Review,** XXXII (1952).

Branda, Eldon S. "Portrait of a Cowboy as a Young Artist," **Southwestern Historical Quarterly,** LXXI (July, 1967).

"Branding Cattle on the Prairies of Texas," **Leslie's Illustrated,** June 25, 1867.

"Breaking a Mustang in California," **Leslie's Illustrated,** October 10, 1874.

Case, Perry. "The Long Drive," **American Heritage,** XI (April, 1960).

"Cattle Branding in New Mexico," **Leslie's Illustrated,** August 15, 1874.

"Cattle in a Western Blizzard," **Harper's Weekly,** February 27, 1886.

"A Colorado 'Dug-Out,'" **Harper's Weekly,** November 18, 1882.

Cook, James H. "The Texas Trail," **Nebraska History Magazine,** XVI (October-December, 1935).

"The 'Cow Boys' of Arizona," **Harper's Weekly,** February 25, 1882.

"Cowboy at Work," **Leslie's Illustrated,** April 30, 1887.

"Cowboy Diversions," **Leslie's Illustrated,** May 5, 1888.

"Cowboys in Wyoming," **Leslie's Illustrated,** November 3, 1888.

Davis, Ronald L. "Soiled Doves and Ornamental Culture," **The American West,** IV (November, 1967).

"Driving Cattle into a Corral," **Harper's Weekly,** Supplement, September 11, 1975.

"Effects of the Loco Weed," **Leslie's Illustrated,** January 23, 1892.

"Erasing Cattle Brands," **Great Falls Tribune,** March 13, 1886.

Frantz, Joe B. "Hoof and Horn on the Chisholm Trail," **The American West,** IV (August, 1967).

Gard, Wayne. "The Impact of the Cattle Trails," **Southwestern Historical Quarterly,** LXXI (July, 1967).

Jordan, Terry G. "The Origin of Anglo-American Cattle Ranching in Texas: A Documentation of Diffusion from the Lower South," **Economic Geography,** XLV (January, 1969).

Josephy, Alvin M., Jr. "First 'Dude Ranch' Trip to the Untamed West," **American Heritage,** VII (February, 1956).

Harger, Charles M. "Cattle-Trails of the Prairies," **Scribner's Magazine,** XI (June, 1892).

"How the Texas Cow-Boy Lives," **Victoria** (Texas) **Advocate,** January 5, 1878.

Hutchinson, William H. "The Cowboy and the Class Struggle (or, Never Put Marx in the Saddle)," **Arizona and the West,** XIV (Winter, 1972).

"The Last Drive," **Great Falls Tribune** (Semi-Weekly), July 30, 1887.

McKeen, Ona Lee. "The Cowhand," **American Heritage,** XIV (October, 1963).

"Memories," **Puck,** October 8, 1913.

Metzger, S. S. "A Day With the Round-Up," **Pacific Monthly,** July, 1911.

Miller, C. R. "How Texas Handles Cattle," **Leslie's Illustrated,** January 25, 1906.

Noel, Leon. "The Largest Estate in the World," **Overland Monthly,** Second Series, XII (November, 1888).

Olstad, Charles F. "The 'Wild West' in Spain," **Arizona and the West,** VI (Autumn, 1964).

"The Pioneer Cattle Drive," **Great Falls Tribune,** June 25, 1885.

Porter, Kenneth W. "Negro Labor in the Western Cattle Industry," **Labor History,** X (Summer, 1969).

"Raising Supplies of Meats for Foreign Markets," **Leslie's Illustrated,** July 27, 1878.

Rodnitzky, Jerome L. "Recapturing the West: The Dude Ranch in American Life," **Arizona and the West,** X (Summer, 1968).

Sanderlin, Walter S. Ed. "A Cattle Drive from Texas to California: The Diary of M. H. Erskine, 1854," **Southwestern Historical Quarterly,** LXVII (January, 1964).

Smith, Helena Huntington. "The Rise and Fall of Alex Swan," **The American West,** IV (August, 1967).

"Some Facts About Cow-Boys," **Harper's Weekly,** October 16, 1886.

"A Stampede in New Mexico," **Leslie's Illustrated,** May 12, 1877.

"Texas Cattle-Drive," **Great Falls Tribune,** March 27, 1886.

"Texas Cattle Raising," **Harper's Weekly,** October 19, 1867.

"The Texas Cow-Boy," **Leslie's Illustrated,** December 1, 1883.

"The Texas Cow-Boy," **Victoria** (Texas) **Advocate,** April 12, 1879.

"Texas Cowboys on a Holiday Excursion," **Leslie's Illustrated,** January 14, 1882.

"Texas Cowboys on a Lark," **Leslie's Illustrated,** January 17, 1885.

"Things in and About San Antonio," **Leslie's Illustrated,** January 15, 1859.

Tripplett, J. F. "The Scout's Story: From the Journal of a Cattleman," **The Atlantic Monthly,** CXXXV (April, 1925).

"Vocational Education," **Time,** LXXXVII (June 10, 1966).

Williams, Eugene. "The Cattle Roundup," **The Colorado Magazine,** V (October, 1928).

index

251